T0196530

BIRTHING A
DREAM

How to Achieve Your Dreams: from Conception to Birth

Aaron Womack Jr.

BIRTHING A DREAM
HOW TO ACHIEVE YOUR DREAMS: FROM CONCEPTION TO BIRTH

Scripture quotations marked KJV are from the Holy Bible, King James Version (Authorized Version). First published in 1611. Quoted from the KJV Classic Reference Bible, Copyright © 1983 by The Zondervan Corporation.

iUniverse books may be ordered through booksellers or by contacting:

iUniverse
1663 Liberty Drive
Bloomington, IN 47403
www.iuniverse.com
1-800-Authors (1-800-288-4677)

Because of the dynamic nature of the Internet, any web addresses or links contained in this book may have changed since publication and may no longer be valid. The views expressed in this work are solely those of the author and do not necessarily reflect the views of the publisher, and the publisher hereby disclaims any responsibility for them.

Any people depicted in stock imagery provided by Getty Images are models, and such images are being used for illustrative purposes only. Certain stock imagery © Getty Images.

ISBN: 978-1-5320-5533-1 (sc)
ISBN: 978-1-5320-5534-8 (e)

Library of Congress Control Number: 2018909973

Print information available on the last page.

iUniverse rev. date: 08/24/2018

Contents

Foreword

I am pleased to call Aaron Womack Jr., affectionately known to his friends as "A Train" or simply "Train" because of his prodigious 6'8" frame, both friend and confidant. We first met 22 years ago when, after seeing him coach, I convinced him to assist me in coaching basketball at a local Milwaukee prep school. Over the years, he coached for me, we coached as equals, and I coached for him. With each passing year, our friendship and respect for each other has steadily grown. Aaron is a husband, father, and family man, award winning teacher, successful coach, school administrator, part-time pastor, and a motivator extraordinaire. What is most striking and memorable about him, though, is his tremendous sense of humor and positive, infectious can-do attitude. Everyone who meets him or knows him is drawn to his magnetic personality, broad grin, and hearty laugh.

There is one insight into Aaron that I think shows the true measure of his character and work ethic. This is a man who never started a high school basketball game in his career and, yet, he would go on to earn a Division I scholarship, start for his team in Junior College, and be a part of two NCAA tournaments teams! He is a person who preaches the power of positive thinking and constant personal improvement because he has lived it and practiced it his whole life. What you are about to read is a compilation of wisdom, humor, and motivational insight that is equally applicable to student, athlete, doctor, CEO, or anyone looking for a positive path forward. I recommend this book highly and know that you will benefit by reading it.

Dave Liccione
Milwaukee, Wisconsin

Prologue

It began as an ordinary Saturday evening, until the ordinary turned extraordinary. As usual on game day I couldn't sleep the night before with my mind thinking about a thousand different things I should have done better or differently in preparation for our game against DeKalb High School that Saturday night. This would be our third year in a row facing this team and we had established somewhat of a rivalry, a friendly competitive one.

DeKalb was about a two-hour drive from Milwaukee Madison High School, the home of the Knights and a team I had been coaching for four years. I knew their team would be getting to our gym a little early and I had some things to take care of before they arrived as I wouldn't get a chance later because when DeKalb arrived I would spend some time with their coach, talking and catching up with my new friend. It's nice and yet tough to compete and try to win against someone you know, like, and respect.

Game time was a little earlier than most Varsity contests and it was set up this way deliberately as DeKalb had to endure the long trip back. We won our first contest against them at our place and they had taken the victory the next year at their place. Since Northern Illinois University is located in DeKalb we took advantage of our trip there the year before and stayed overnight. This gave us a chance to take a college tour of Northern Illinois and have an opportunity to watch part of their men's basketball team practice. Their coach, Ricardo Patton, was even gracious enough to talk to our players. Coach Patton said a lot of good things, but what stood out to me most was when he said, "Don't say hello, when it's time to say goodbye."

This meant, put in the necessary work before you become a senior and are getting ready to say goodbye. Coach Patton said that he seen so many seniors want to visit the weight room for the first time, study film on their own for the first time, or visit the library for the first time during their last year. Say hello to these things before it's time to say goodbye.

About three hours before the Saturday evening upon I was saying hello to the washing machine, I was washing our freshmen, junior varsity, and varsity team uniforms. We were fortunate to have 3 sets of uniforms just for the varsity alone, but I made sure to collect them after every game so that my staff and I could rotate washing them to make sure we got them back in time for each game and that they stayed as new as possible. I don't know if it was my turn to wash but since I was up all night and couldn't get a nap in, I might as well get started on them.

I had just finish the first load, put the next load in and started to hang the wet ones because I couldn't take a chance of drying them. I scolded myself for not bringing enough hangers to the laundry room, I left to retrieve some more. As I entered the hallway my phone rang, I said hello but there wasn't an answer. Its game day so I didn't have time to talk to whomever it was and if it was really important they'd call back. Then realizing that it could be Coach Rohlman saying that there was delay in their arrival or something I checked the number. Noticing that I had missed eight calls from the same number, all in a row, I remembered that in the back laundry room my cell phone didn't have good reception. I also didn't have all of my contacts listed by name either, so I didn't know who the phone number belonged to. I called the number back and one of my coaches, Kevin Johnikin answered. I figured he wanted to check on the game coming up since it was his relationship with the DeKalb staff that got us started playing each other. Or he could have been calling to try and calm my nerves.

"Hello," Johnikin said.

"Hey man, what's up? Sorry I missed your call, I was in the back doing laundry and you know the reception is bad in there."

"Hey, where are you now?"

"Headed to the locker room to get some hangers," I said.

"You need to sit down."

I laughed. "I'm good man, I know you think I'm real nervous, but I'm not any more nervous than the usual. I'm fine coach, just need to…."

"Naw man, have a seat, I need to tell you something."

Not liking the tone in his voice I said, "Dang man, you good? What's up?'

"I got some bad news. Johntel lost his mother just a little while ago. I've been at the hospital and he's not taking it well."

"What! Oh, no. Where are you?"

"St. Joseph's." St. Joseph's is what's known as the baby hospital in Milwaukee located on Burleigh Street. It's where my youngest was born as well as all of my siblings and where I was taken after I was born at home.

"I'm on my way."

Johntel is Johntel Franklin. Johntel was a football player playing basketball and not only a really good athlete, but an all-around great person. His mom had been diagnosed with cancer, but was thought to be in remission. His father wasn't around so his mom raised him and his sibling. In spite of that, Johntel maintained a good standing in school and was being recruited by a number of colleges. Any other big time athlete in another sport would have skipped their senior year in the sport they're not as noteworthy in. But knowing the team could use his help, and the fact that he has been a starter on varsity since his sophomore season, kept him going out for basketball.

On my way to the hospital I kept going over and over in my head what I could possibly say to him to add some sort of comfort. This young seventeen-year-old kid was suddenly without basically the only parent he had known. Where was he going to go, who was going to continue to raise him, who would provide food and shelter? Who was going to be his momma?

After calling my other coaches and telling them what was taking place I informed them that I would be at the hospital for a while and that they are to get things started and I would be there later.

There was a junior varsity game before the varsity game and I already figured I would be cutting it close if I was going to make the start of the varsity game. I wasn't worried about making the pregame and going over all the things that needed to be taken care before a game because I had very capable and trustworthy assistants. Besides Coach Johnikin, there was Sam Guyton, head coach of the junior varsity, who was more than capable of running his own program and Kenny Green, he coached the freshmen team and I knew he would work in tandem with Sam to prepare the varsity as the junior varsity team finished their game.

Everyone knew the important keys to the game and it was just a matter of what type of speech they would give. This speech could not be the usual rah, rah, as the coaches had to deliver the news to some of the players that hadn't already heard the news of Johntel's mother. I knew the news had spread to this tight knit group because when I arrived at the hospital one of my other players, Johntel's good friend and teammate, Josh Brown was already there. I was not prepared for the atmosphere there. Just seeing the tears on Johntel's and Josh's face brought me to tears. Other teammates wanted to come, but they were waiting to go in shifts. After talking to the family, I was able to catch some alone time with Johntel and Josh. The conversation ended up coming to a question of should we play the game or not. I didn't want the team from DeKalb to have to travel all the way back home without a game, but my mind wasn't in it, and neither were the two players with me.

As I made preparations to call Sam and have him whole heartily apologize to the DeKalb team and let them know that under the circumstances we wouldn't be playing the game, Johntel stood up and said, "Hang the phone up coach."

After being silent for what seemed like an eternity, Josh said, "Bro what are you talking about? We can't play this game."

"Yes you can. Not only is the game going to be played, but Josh, you're playing and the rest of you are going to win it......for my mom." More tears.

Josh and Johntel went back and forth about the merits of playing the game and not playing. I was in a daze until Sam' voice snapped me out of a trace. He was screaming on the phone, what do you want me to do, cancel the game or play?

"Hello, Sam, yeah, Johntel said he wants the game to go on."

"Is he sure?"

"Are you sure Johntel, play the game?"

"Yeah, and Josh is playing also."

A little more arguing took place and Josh finally relented and after his sister picked him up, he headed to the game. Johntel said he appreciated the jester of being willing to cancel, but not playing the game wouldn't bring his mother back and that the team had traveled so far. I sat back down and told him whatever he needed I would do. He then asked me something incredible. He then asked me to leave, to get to the gym and get the guys ready to play their hearts out.

"Johntel, I can't go."

"The team worked so hard all week to get ready for the game."

"Johntel, I can't go."

"We lost to them last year and now we need revenge."

"Johntel, I can't go."

"If we don't play, tonight, we may never get this chance to play again."

Johntel, I can't go."

"Losing my mom made we realize the greatest gift we have in life."

"Johntel, I can't go."

"The greatest gift we have is the present. Tomorrow is not guaranteed and they need to play. GO!"

On my way to the gym my head was filled with guilt for going to the game. Did I care more about the game than his feelings, his situation? But if this is what he wanted, then I had to oblige. I wasn't aware of the time or what I had to do to get prepared for the game: pregame rituals, keys to the game, starting lineups with Johntel out, who would take his place, etc. I had enough to just try and focus on the traffic. I called Sam before I left the hospital and told him to get the players ready. Make sure the scorebook was accurate but to leave Johntel out, he wasn't going to play but would certainly be rooting for us. Sam asked about Josh and I told him that he was going to play because Johntel was making him. The last thing I heard before he hung up was that Josh wasn't at the gym yet, funny because he had left over an hour ago.

It wasn't until I arrived at the gym and saw the charter bus for the DeKalb team that I began to realize we had a game to play. It was then that I checked my watch and came to grasp what time it was. I must have spent more time at the hospital then I anticipated. It was an hour after the time that the game should have started so both teams should just be coming out of the locker room getting ready for the second half. As I said before I had an excellent coaching staff, I knew that everything would be taken care. I had planned to just go sit on the bench and become a cheerleader. Part of me kept saying, the game doesn't matter, but the competitor in me said, I hope we're winning. Before I got to the door I made a vow to myself that if we are losing I wouldn't interfere, just let Sam coach and I would be his assistant tonight.

I entered the building and was greeted by security. "Hey coach, sorry to hear about Johntel's mom, how's he doing?"

"About as well as expected. He's still at the hospital."

"Yeah, I know, Coach Johnikin just left out of here a few minutes ago, said Johntel called him and he was headed back over to the hospital."

I wondered what that was about, maybe he still needed more support; I shouldn't have left him. Now some more guilt kicked in. I should just turn around and leave. I decided to at least wait until after the game, so that I could speak to Coach Rohlman.

"Coach, you alright," said one of the security?

I didn't realize I was just standing there in a daze. "Yeah, I'm good, thanks. Talk to ya'll later."

"Okay, coach, good luck."

"Thanks."

Still in a daze I entered the gym. Our bench was closest to the door I was entering and so was the visitor's locker room. Not wanting to run into the DeKalb team as they might be heading back out onto the court after halftime, I turned back around and asked the usher by the door if DeKalb was back out on the floor yet. She said, yes they've been there for quite a while. Not realizing what she was talking about, I took off my coat and prepared to make my way to the bench. I was going to sneak a seat on the end and try not to cause a commotion.

But when I came in something felt strange. I saw both teams warming up, that wasn't strange as teams do that after halftime. I saw the referees standing by the scorer's table, that wasn't strange. My team was looking somber, that was to be expected. What I didn't expect was that the crowd was sitting and quiet. What I didn't expect was Coach Rolhman and his staff at near center court. What I didn't expect was seeing the score board and with no time running down to dictate that halftime was ending. What I didn't expect was that neither team seemed to have scored any points as both teams had "0's" posted.

Then I see the entire gym looking at me. I walked toward Coach Rohlman and asked Sam what was going on. When DeKalb heard about what happened with Johntel they wanted to wait to see if the game was going to be played. When they heard it was going to be played, they said they wanted to wait for me to get back. I asked Sam why he didn't tell them that the game could get started without me. I was told that DeKalb said they would wait no matter what. Unbelievable, knowing they had a two-hour bus ride waiting for them after the game they still waited.

They had warmed up and then went to the locker room and warmed up again and then sat down and warmed up again. After telling DeKalb's coach that he didn't have to do that and thanking him profusely he said it was either playing the game or heading over to the hospital and sit there with the entire team. Knowing he could have won the game by forfeit it didn't keep him from waiting.

I turned to get my team ready and as I was talking to the players, Josh Brown came running into the gym. I would learn later that after he supposedly left the hospital he didn't really leave. He said he just couldn't leave and kept going back to the hospital. The game would start about two hours after it was supposed to. Josh wouldn't start at his usual point guard position because he was still getting dressed and had to warmup.

Surprisingly my team had shaken off their somber faces and had come out playing quite well despite missing two starters from the lineup against a good DeKalb team that had two players being recruited in their starting lineup with one player being a good post player that was most certainly a division one college player. We were up by five when Josh was ready to enter the game. DeKalb took the lead back with an 8 to 0 run as their nice, but competitive coach, went after a good but certainly stiff and not yet lose Josh Brown. My guys fought back and we were up by 5 at the end of the first quarter.

The start of the second quarter was much like the start of the game with my team coming out playing and fighting hard. I was happy to be up by double digits but felt bad for having to play a team that stayed around two additional hours and never complained about it. My feelings of being sorry quickly faded when DeKalb cut the lead to two. A close game had my mind back to coaching and becoming the predator and going into attack mode and trying to do whatever it took to win. Competition will do that to you.

Having our lead cut to two, I was being yelled at by Sam to call a timeout. I like to have my guys' figure things out and save timeouts for the end of the game. As I got ready to yell back, we have a relationship like that, something caught the corner of my eye. Could it be, no way, wait, yes it is.

"Timeout."

This was not a timeout to talk strategy. As the players made their way to the bench they saw what the timeout was about and ran to the end of the bench. The crowd then saw what the timeout was about and stood to their feet. The DeKalb team also began to realize what the timeout was about and made their way to our bench. Remarkably, Johntel had come into the gym. Hugs, high fives, and a standing ovation had the gym on pause again. The referees had understood as they allowed us to have the longest timeout I had ever been a part of.

Time to get back to work, time to get back to try and win this game. Johntel had come and gave his ultimate blessing for playing the game by unselfishly showing up and cheering us on. At least that's what I thought he was doing when Coach Johnikin came behind me and whispered that he, Johntel, wanted to play. The human side of me would have been delighted to have him play, the competitor side of me said oh no, he can't, he's not in the scorer's book and thus by entering him after the game has started meant a two shot technical foul shot awarded to DeKalb, which means in a close game, it could be the difference between winning and losing.

When I looked down the bench and saw the look on his face, I had no choice but to yell, "Hurry up, and get dressed." He rushed into the locker room but came back out without his uniform. He couldn't find his uniform; it wasn't hanging up where it was supposed to be. I couldn't remember if I had left it in the laundry room or if it was hanging in the drying room or if I had washed it at all. I didn't have time to stop the game and check. But it was Johntel, so Sam could take over as I left to go look. I'll be right back, do I need to call another timeout, dang, DeKalb just stole the ball and scored again, we're tied up.

I didn't have time to go look or give directions, I had to…

"Coach, he can have my uni."

Before I could tell who said what, one of the reserve players was striping off his uniform and giving it to Johntel. Now it was a matter of subbing him in the game. Once Johntel was at the scorer's table I let the table and referee know that I was aware that it would be a two shot technical. Johntel entered the gym to another standing ovation. One of the referees went to explain that a technical shot would be given and asked who DeKalb wanted to shoot the shot. I could hear their coach arguing that he didn't want the technical and the referee insisting that one had to be taken. After watching the referee and coach go back and forth for a little bit I turned to talk to my team. We had to work on possibly being down two after they sent their best foul shooter to the line and them having the ball taken out of bounds as well. No problem, we'd been in worst situations and we could handle it. Here comes the first shot by their best shooter…. wow he air balled that shot. It didn't hit rim and it almost rolled to the wall.

I can't believe they sent a bad shooter to the free throw line. That's what I was thinking at first, but they didn't. At the line was their starting point guard, he's not only a good player, but a good foul shooter as well. I turned from my huddle to watch him shoot the next one. This time the ball rolled even shorter of its mark, it seemed as he was bowling instead of shooting a foul shot. Then I knew that he had missed the shots on purpose and I had my players stand and applaud their team for a great show of sportsmanship.

I would later find out that when the Coach Rohlman sent his player to the line he said to him, you know you're going to miss these shots, right? The player said he knew. Missing the shot would lower his 80% shooting average. By lowering his percentage, he and the team raised something more. They raised sportsmanship and the essence of playing for more than just a game to another level.

I was so moved that I wrote a letter to the School District of DeKalb. They forwarded the letter to the local newspaper and the story was picked up by a national publication and various national radio stations. It then reached ABC World News Tonight and ESPN's own Tom Rinaldi came all the way to Milwaukee to do a story live.

Introduction

As the news of what took place that extraordinary Saturday evening began to spread, I received hundreds of phone calls, emails, texts from strangers and friends alike. I had been interrupted in my teaching classroom throughout all times of the day. The secretary at my school would tell them that I was teaching and that she didn't want to disturb me, but when the person on the other line said they were from ABC, CBS, NBC, connected to television or radio, the call amazingly went through. ABC News made our team the story of the week on the national evening news. Radio stations from around the country wanted to get me live on the air, it was hard for our secretary not to at least ask if I was available.

I met so many interesting people through all types of correspondents, and I tried to answer every email, text, letter, or phone call. In talking with many people it seemed that a recurring theme kept being asked. What made Johntell so dedicated, so committed to the team that he chose to come and play that night? Not only that, but what made Coach Rohlman so committed, not to the game, but to the friendship we had established, that he was willing to stay and wait even after two hours. Even more so, to see how Johntell was doing and then was still willing to play the game, and to not take a penalty that was rightfully afforded to his team?

It made me think about commitment. What does it mean, how can you get it, is it something you're born with or is it something you can develop? What does it look like and is it easily recognizable? How can some have it and others not have it? How can people in a profession or on the same team or within the same family have it, yet the person next to them not? What about successful people? Do all successful people have commitment before becoming successful or do they get committed after achieving success? Are there levels to commitment and if so, what are those levels of commitment?

Since this event took place, I became curious enough about commitment that I launched the exploration of the idea surrounding commitment. Is it something that's attainable, is it real, can it be touched or is it just a cliche that was created by someone years ago? In trying to find out about commitment I believed it had to be a foundation that you must have in order to achieve goals and dreams. I wanted to start with reaching goals and dreams because it's something I had thought about and talked about for years. Thus, I went about the task of studying commitment.

I began by reflecting on my own life. After teaching in the Milwaukee School Public School system for over twenty years, being a supporting teacher and an administrator for over four years, I had developed my own idea about commitment. Not just as a definition, but how it can be brought to life. I have coached boys' and men's basketball in various levels for over twenty years as well. But I didn't want to just rely on my own experiences to determine what commitment was or is. So I began to study athletes, people in other professions near and far. I didn't study them as much as just observed them. I did this over the years for my own curiosity. I didn't do this for the sole purpose of writing a book. That didn't come to me until years later when people continued to ask me to speak to different groups for various occasions.

Why was I committed to talk to some groups and not others? In reflecting over my life, I came to understand what commitment really was in my own terms and I tried to put a handle on why I demonstrated commitment sometimes and not at other times. I explored the results of what happened when I was committed to something and what took place that served as factors when I wasn't. How did my commitment or lack thereof lead to accomplishing my goals or failing to reach them? With that in mind, I tried to find other working definitions of commitment by so called experts. I watched endless hours of tapes, read thousands upon thousands of pages of books and have been a listener to many motivational speakers. I compiled some of the things I heard, "borrowed" some good ideas and decided to embrace my idea about commitment and how it can be an essential ingredient to make you a success. Hence, this book was formed.

This book is my attempt to do something more than to say to you the reader, "Hey, in order to be successful and reach your dreams you have to be committed to it." That's cool and all, but I wanted it to be much more than that. I didn't want to just say that as a theme and then show examples of people having commitment. This book is not about saying as long as you're committed to your cause, you will be instantly successful. In this book I will put commitment into perspective and will make it come alive for you.

This is not a self-help book, but more of an account of my personal journey in examining my experiences to learn what it takes for me to be committed to achieve my goals and dreams. I have had enough failed experiences and bouts with procrastination to realize that times when I believed I was truly committed were times when I actually was only partially in. As I looked into these specific time periods I began to notice that success for me happened in stages and the work I needed to put in to achieve my goal took on an average nine months for me to see success. The nine months really stood out to me and I realized the same amount of time was the average time needed for a woman to go from pregnancy to birth. The stages I needed to work through to achieve my goals were also parallel to the three stages or trimesters of a woman's pregnancy. Now I don't claim to be an expert on pregnancy, even though I am a dad, but since I began this personal journey I have found multiple similarities between the two and the commitment it takes which I will share throughout this book.

Shaka Smart, basketball coach at the University of Texas, talks about the difference between those that are interested in something and those that are committed to something in an article I read a while ago. He said if you're interested in something, you do something when you feel like it. But if you're committed to something, you do it regardless.

With that in mind, this book makes the connection of being pregnant as an example of showing commitment. A woman can't decide to simply say, I'm tired, I'm going to have my husband, or my sister, or brother carry my baby today. Once a woman has made that commitment to pregnancy she carries that commitment to full term. If we are to be fully committed to an endeavor, we have to show the same commitment. I will take you through the essence of a nine-month pregnancy and show you what to expect at the full term of your pregnancy commitment.

It's exciting to come to the realization of what your passion is and how you're going to go about achieving your passion. It's easy to want to just go full force at it and work until you finally give up. Not having the success you want doesn't mean you haven't chosen the right path in life, it could simply mean you made the same mistake that I and many others have done, you jumped into something without much thought or planning. In getting pregnant you will come to understand that gifts, like a child, take time to develop. It takes time and a proper diagnosis, you're either nurturing something or destroying it, and sometimes your gifts can be hidden.

In writing this book, I have researched successful people and it became therapeutic for me to identify my levels of commitment needed to goals I wanted to achieve. The times when I did not achieve something can be attributed to many factors, but once I examined my level of commitment, I determined I could have overcome some of those factors. Whether you are waiting for you dreams to come true, have experienced the success you wanted, or don't know how to get started, this book is for you. No matter what your age, you're never too old to jump start your dreams. No matter your age, you're never too old to become pregnant. Are you ready?

FIRST
TRIMESTER

1

"Diligence is the mother of good luck." – Benjamin Franklin

We are lucky while surrounded by failure. My parents are failures; both of them. My mom is a failure and so is my dad. It wasn't until I became an adult that I realized that they were failures. In fact, it wasn't until I had turned forty that I found out what a failure my father had been. My uncle, my dad's brother, delivered the news to me. He told me about a restaurant that was located on a cross section of town in Jackson, Tennessee. My dad was from the country where on any given night he and his cousins would sneak and borrow the "mule" their family had for a night out on the town. Nowadays it would translate into the taking of the family car. While in town my dad, uncle and a couple of cousins would frequent this particular restaurant where Blacks were allowed to eat, but only in the kitchen and only if they entered into the kitchen through the back of the restaurant.

Knowing this wasn't right, even though it was the sign of the times in the 50's, my dad was determined to get the entrance policy changed, but failed many times in trying to get it changed. His failures led him to buck the trend and simply enter in through the front of the restaurant. He didn't make an announcement to the guys about what he was about to do. He simply did it. My uncle told me the first time it happened he didn't notice until he got to the back of the restaurant and saw my dad was missing along with a cousin, nicknamed Bird. This had to have been a scary feeling in the South as Blacks had been known to just disappear and never to be heard from again. The crew that was entering from the back came back to the front just in time to see my dad and Bird getting kicked out the restaurant and being told to go to the back door. My dad, having failed at his first attempt, couldn't help himself. Failing once does not make you a failure. So he had to fail again, which he did, over and over again.

He kept walking in through the front of that restaurant, even after being scolded by my uncle and other cousins and even being told that he was going to get them killed. However, the two front door party members slowly turned into three, and then four, and then the rest of the crew that came with them. My failing father, who was willing to fail to adhere to racist views, was met again by a waitress' protest, but this time the owner said to just let them in and have a seat. Failure doesn't just happen once; it may happen over and over again. Results happen when you become a persistent failure.

After much probing again, I found out that my dad was also the first to integrate a lunch counter at the downtown Woolworth store. I asked him why he persistently ate there knowing that someone in the back had probably spit on his food. He simply said someone had to get things started. I wondered why my parents never mentioned these life-altering experiences to me or my sisters. Was it because many things that we do in life are not to be sought out for attention but are instead just doing what is right and just? Our purpose or determination to fight for what is right is often innate and part of who you are; it is part of your DNA. Often in the early stages of a woman's pregnancy, she may not even know she is pregnant, and it definitely can't be seen by others. However, when the woman finds out she is pregnant she now has a new purpose or commitment. You can determine your purpose by what you are committed to. This will be discussed more in the next chapter.

My mom, being a part of a family whose siblings never went to college failed to make that her fate. She had dreamed of going to college since she was a little girl. In order to change that, she failed to have the normal childhood that others her age could enjoy. She went to work when she was in the 3rd and 4th grade. She received $3 dollars a day for chopping cotton and 25 cents a day for picking it. This was back breaking, grueling work for an adult let alone a child. That wasn't all; she also picked strawberries and was paid 25 cents a quart and 50 cents a quart if they were capped (if you're not sure what capping strawberries mean, ask someone). My mom was allowed to buy back the ones they picked for 15 cents a quart to take home.

She worked those jobs until she reached the 8th grade. She then started working as a housekeeper. She worked as a housekeeper in the household that her mother, my grandmother worked. She was now responsible for washing clothes, cooking, cleaning and serving as a nanny to the children in the house. Even though these children were older than her, she had more responsibility than they did. She stepped in and completed that work because my grandmother was getting too old to work that type of job. My mother continued in this job until she eventually began working for the children of the household who were now grown. My failing mother was able to go to college by remaining on the job. To make sure money for school didn't run short, she went with the family to Mexico for 3 months to tend to the children of her employer. She left her family and friends to stay in a foreign country she had never visited. She was pregnant, committed, about going to school. This pregnancy showed great courage and tenacity.

While my siblings and I were growing up, my mom would often fail to eat or wear the newest best clothing so that her kids could have what she wanted to them to have. In order to be successful you have to experience persistent failure which will lead you to sacrifice. By sacrifice, I mean, passing on going to see that newly released movie, and waiting to see it when it comes out on Netflix, or passing on getting the newest updated cell phone or even passing on sleep. When you become pregnant you fail to worry about not only what others think, but you fail to worry only about yourself and how you look to others. In the beginning, pregnant women may want to look good and get the latest and greatest maternity clothes, but as you start to develop your commitment more, you're keeping up with the Jones' doesn't matter.

If you're going to commit to the point of pregnancy with your dreams you must embrace the first step, failure. If you're afraid of failure, you might as well stop reading now. Give this book to someone else that is ready to get started. I'm not just talking about failing from a standpoint of someone telling you "no" when you're trying to sell them something or hearing "no" when you just finished interviewing for that job you wanted. Those failures are small potatoes. I'm talking about embracing failure in such a way that you chase after failure, you seek it out. Those people that haven't failed at something or haven't had a lot of people talk negatively about them are most likely not doing anything.

Be comfortable and surround yourself with failure. You are here by luck. Again I say we are lucky while surrounded by failure. You, I, all of us came about as a result of failure. When your parents got together, over 400 million sperm were released, not all of them made it. It only takes one sperm to fertilize an egg. Sometimes multiple eggs are fertilized but an over whelming amount fail. I'm glad the other sperms failed, otherwise I wouldn't be here. Embracing failure should be a part of our DNA. Successful people don't run from failure, they seek it, go after it. When one thing is accomplished, it's time to fail at something else. If you're not willing to seek failure, to go after it, you're not willing to be committed. It's as simple as that. Does this mean to purposely do something you know you can't do, no? I know I can't be a doctor. You can tell me I can be anything I put my mind to, but having to spend over eight years of graduate school to look at blood would never do it for me.

Sara Blakely, who is the founder of Spanx, knows about failure. She has made it her friend. According to her interview on the news show "60 Minutes", in less than ten years, she became the youngest self-made billionaire. She has never taken a business class and does not have the experience most would need in her field. However, she states that she is a grade "A" student when it comes to not accepting "no" for an answer. She was set to go to law school and took the LSAT test, but she failed it. After that set back, she started selling computers. In those days computers were big and bulky, and she had to take them door to door. Failure started for Sara when she and her brother were young. At the dinner table her father would ask them what they had failed at for the week. He planted seeds in them that if they didn't fail at something, they weren't trying enough new things.

While getting together to go out with her friends, she thought why hadn't **someone** invented something so that some of her body parts could be sucked in and didn't have to stick out. She became that someone, but failure was still within her reach. The product was invented, but had not been sold yet. Just because she came up with the idea of a product no one handed her one hundred million dollars to make her dream come true. She still had to sell the idea, the product, and then herself, and do this with no formal planning, no business plan or knowledge about marketing. She did have a desire to fail. She failed her way into a department store and tried to convince people to buy her product. Her display was not in the greatest location to be seen, again, another failure. She failed her way to a chance meeting with Oprah Winfrey, who mentioned that she liked the product and suddenly sales multiplied, another example of a persistent failure.

Failure was no stranger to Michael Jordan either. Jordan, arguably the greatest basketball player of all time, could have just retired as the greatest. He didn't have to retire from basketball to try his hand at baseball, but he sought out failure. Because of his desire to take a risk and try something new, he was laughed at and had articles written about him to quit baseball because he was embarrassing himself. He didn't let failure bother him.

Michael Jordan has stated numerous times in interviews and commercials that he failed at making the varsity team as a sophomore, his team failed to win a second championship in college even though he was on one of the most talented teams after his freshman year. He failed to become an NBA Champion with his first two coaches in the league. Even after winning 6 championships he failed to get his General Manager (GM) to believe he was a major part of those championships. The GM at the time, Jerry Krause said publicly that "Players don't win championships, organizations do." Failure led him to become the General Manager of the Washington Wizards and eventually getting fired from that position. Failure led him to try again as a General Manager with the Charlotte Bobcats where he then became part owner and later, a majority owner. His comfort in being a persistent failure led him to be more successful off the court than on it, which was hard to do considering all of his success on the court.

It is because of my parents willing to be failures that have help lead them to be successful and allowed my siblings and me to have things others couldn't or didn't have. My parents have accomplished many things in their lifetime, many things that I am extremely proud of and have taught us great lessons in life that were not taught in school. The greatest of them all was not to let the potential of failure keep us from doing somethings. We were taught, learning from your failures is experience, and learning from other's failures is wisdom.

2

Conception

"If you don't pay the price for success you pay the price for failure." Zig Ziglar

Once you've accepted that failure is a part of being committed you're ready to become pregnant. Being pregnant is showing your commitment. Some experts on commitment talk about there being one level of commitment while others talk about different levels of commitment. Some things you are a little more committed to than others. You may be committed to your goal of writing a book. You sit down and write, you stick to what you set your goals to be, you just do it. Maybe your goal is to set out and write a few pages or chapters a day. You do this diligently for the first five days but you just can't write on day six because you can't write and do the other things you may have committed to. Maybe you're committed to heading out of town with the guys or a trip with the girls?

Which one do you do? If you're going to be committed with the commitment of being pregnant with your goals, if this goal is your baby growing inside of you, then you can't be a little committed to this and a lot committed to that. You can't be a little pregnant, you either are or you aren't. You are pregnant with this goal or dream that you're going to be working on, then that is it, period. Now, this doesn't mean you can't do other things. Yes, you can take trips or go on shopping sprees, just understand that this baby is going with you. If you are in training to run a marathon, then wherever you go you better make sure a gym is available or there is a place to run. If you're writing, then the laptop comes with you. This is your baby you're carrying; plan accordingly.

According to research, of the ten things highly successful people do, one thing they don't do is multitask. I know this might sound different than other people's perception, but being the jack of all trades and the master of none won't cut it. The other thing about pregnancy is once you're pregnant you can't get pregnant again until you give birth. You can have multiple births but there is only one pregnancy. You have to have one goal you're committed to. I tried to do multiple things and be committed to all of them and I missed out on all marks. When I decided to become a motivational speaker, I committed myself to speaking, writing articles, finding speaking engagements, writing three books, and a host of other things. I was not successful at any, at least not to the level of success I wanted. I couldn't have multiple pregnancies. I had to choose one, the other may become a part of multiple births, but there is still just one pregnancy. Tyler Perry stated in his interview with Oprah Winfrey, part of the reason he made it was because of one focus, he narrowed his focus to one idea. This is one pregnancy.

Once I decided to get impregnated with writing this book, the other things that I wanted became a part of the book. Will Smith, the rapper and actor, in a YouTube interview describes this as having just a Plan A with no Plan B. He said Plan B distracts you from your Plan A. I grew up being told the opposite. I was told you must have a Plan B to fall back on. I believe that I didn't commit fully to my Plan A because I could always do the next thing. With just a Plan A, being told "no", or being called a failure isn't a bother, it's just an opportunity for a second chance.

For those that don't believe what I am saying about having just a Plan A, let me explain it like I do when I'm giving a speech. I often ask if anyone in the audience has a single mom. I then set the scenario - suppose I was single and I met your mom. Your mom and I date for a while and then I decide I want to marry your single mom. I explain to you that I promise to treat your mother like a queen. That I would be undeniably committed to her and I would give her things she could only dream about. With me, she wouldn't have to work a day in her life, I would treat you and your siblings like you were my own and when it was time, I would pay for every one's college education. She would be treated like the first lady of The United States. The only thing is, I'm not sure if our union is going to work out, so I'm keeping my former girl as Plan B. Would that work for you? I wouldn't think so. It is the same thing with having a single pregnancy or single goal.

In order to get pregnant, you have to have conception. In order to conceive, you have to have a partner, you can't be pregnant alone. Not a partner in the sense of a business partner that you run a company with, but a partner in the sense that you can't get pregnant by yourself, this partner is going to push you. You also have to plant a seed and wait until it is fertilized. But it's not enough just to plant a seed. Take a second and read the directions from a bag of grass seed at your local hardware store. Basically, the directions say in order to ensure you get the best results for growth you should do the following:

1. Clear the spot or the area of old debris of dead grass from the area in which you're going to plant.
2. Dig down a little bit and then cover up the new seeds with straw.
3. Water the seeds often.

When you decide to become committed you need to clear away the dead spots in your life. Dead things can't give life. The hanging out at the clubs are dead, the staying up all hours of the night doing unproductive things are dead. In many cases you have to remove some friends or acquaintances in your life that don't bring life to you. Scientists define life or something being alive by three criteria:

1. Respond to stimuli: If you're poked with a pin you should jump or say ouch.
2. Motion or Locomotion: Do you have movement? Are you in the same spot or space mentally or physically as you were last year, two years ago, five years ago?
3. Growth: Growth isn't just about getting taller. Is there something you can do now that you were unable to do previously? Are you alive or need to become alive? I thought I was alive but wasn't growing; now I know why.

The next step is very important, covering up the seeds. Just like a baby being carried inside of a woman, in the early stages of your commitment pregnancy, you need to have your seed buried so that others don't see it. This is a small, but important entity. Some women are very superstitious when it comes to making the announcement about being pregnant. They don't want to tell others about it until after a certain time. This is what you want. The only one that needs to know you are pregnant is your partner or the person that is there to be your cheerleader. They cheer you when you can't see the justification for working harder than before or doing things that are not fun. The seed is buried deep under cover because the seed need to establish attachment. Roots grow underground. Dreams, goals, aspirations, have to take root and turn into commitment before anything can be seen.

This step is crucial because this is going to be one of the hardest parts for achieving your goals. Others see you not as what you're going to be, but as you are or what you used to be. And for some, what you used to be is what you will always be. This is especially true if you're trying to achieve something that has never been done before by your family or closest friends. According to his autobiography, Malcolm X was told by a teacher that he should not aspire to be a lawyer or a doctor because black boys, especially poor ones, don't become that. A friend was told by his own mother that he would never be nothing, never achieve anything, never amount to anything, "Just like his no good daddy."

The "why" people are a major reason why a lot of people get started, but never finish. It is at this stage, the first trimester, more than any other time that we lose our commitment. We lose our desire. One of the most important elements of success is a belief in you. There has to be an unwavering belief that you can succeed. This at times might not make sense not only to others, but to you as well. I'll explain it as a blind preacher once told me, "You have to SEE IT, before you SEE IT, in order to SEE IT. Others around you can't see it. They can't see your dreams; your pregnancy. So at this stage plant your seed by saying what you're going to do just to your "why not" people, and then keep quiet.

What makes this hard is that people don't understand why you're working out because they don't see the results. They don't understand why you cut out watching television because you aren't making straight A's in class anyway. This is why only your partner/cheerleader will pull an all-nighter with you even though they have to get up early the next day. This why your partner/cheerleader will watch the kids at your house while you're out doing research. This is why your partner/cheerleader will make sure you're not smoking or whatever you shouldn't be doing but also check to see how many chapters you got written today. They see what others don't see.

Bishop T.D. Jakes describes it like this in one of his sermons on *The Word Network*. Imagine being at an elegant hotel. The hotel is hosting a great event. You take the elevator down to the lobby and see everyone in tuxedos. It's no big deal except you enter the lobby in a bathing suit. You get funny looks because you don't fit in with what everyone else is wearing. You're not dressed for their occasion but you're dressed for your occasion, your occasion is to head to the pool. You're not dressed for where you are, but you are dressed for where you're going.

The third direction on that bag of grass seed is to water the seeds often. You have to water the new seeds more than you water the other parts of the lawn. Your new commitment/pregnancy needs more of your time and care than the things you used to do. Some people may think of this as needing more time in the day. Successful people know that everyone has the same 24 hours in a day; they just know how to use it better. You don't need more time; you need to make better use of your time. If you used to work 8 hours a day, sleep 8 hours a day, eat and do whatever recreational activity in the other 8 hours, you now need to expend more water or time on your new commitment/pregnancy.

Chart how much time you spend on things that are not productive. I'm not saying that you need to lose sleep to a point that it's not healthy for you, but if you are spending more time on things that will not help you achieve your goal then you're not pregnant. Even while at work, I spend every free moment or quiet moment thinking about this book. Lunch time is always a working lunch.

The conception stage is a danger zone as well. It is dangerous because you have to be aware of preventers. Preventers are the number one reason why people can't get committed and can't get pregnant. The number one preventer is not others that doubt you. The number one preventer, bar none, is you. Let's take a look in the next chapter.

3

"You are the only problem you will ever have and you are the only solution." Bob Proctor

While he was speaking to a group in Australia, motivational speaking guru, Eric Thomas, was asked by a woman how she could overcome her procrastination. He stated that he doesn't believe in procrastination. It's not a matter of procrastination but a matter of some things not being as important as others. He used the following as an example: If you were offered a chance to collect a million dollars from me the next day, and all you would have to do is show up at 5a.m. at a certain location in the morning. Where would you be at 5a.m. the next morning? The woman stated that she would be at that specific spot at 4:59a.m.

Eric Thomas says there is no such thing as procrastination, but some things are just not as important as others. As he explains in his YouTube broadcast, when things become important enough, we get them done. For me this means having a problem is not a problem; it's not having a solution to the problem that is the problem. The hardest solution to a problem is fixing "us" as the solution to the problem. We all have a choice of making something important enough before it becomes important enough on its own. Someone once said "we want to improve our lot in life, but we don't want to improve ourselves."

If there isn't procrastination, then why does it take such a long time to achieve something for some of us or why are we starting and stopping the things we need to do to get goals accomplished, even when the things we want to accomplish are very, very, important to us? Through studying successful people and non-successful people alike, if we're going to liken commitment to being pregnant with our goals, then we have to realize that there are means that keep us from getting pregnant. Birth control comes in many different forms. There are some forms of birth control that can be seen, like the condom. This is easily detected as using a condom is something you can visibly see and can be easily interpreted that the user is someone who does not want to get pregnant. There are some forms of birth control that can't be seen, they are internal forms of birth control. I want to focus on one form of internal birth control, the birth control pill.

The birth control pill is one of the main barriers for not having commitment because it is ingested by the person that needs to be pregnant with their goals. The function of the birth control pill in a nut shell is that it tricks the body into thinking it is already pregnant. How does that work? Remember as I stated earlier, once the body is pregnant, it can't get pregnant again until you give birth. You can have multiple births, but only one pregnancy. I know I have been guilty of taking the birth control pill, it may not necessarily be called procrastination, but I was tricking my body into thinking that I was working or producing something. Instead of actually writing I would watch television or read a book for pleasure and pretend it was research. I was coming up with different excuses as to why I didn't get something done or placing myself in surroundings that was not conducive to achieving anything.

When I couldn't see the results of working out, even though I worked out every day, I thought it just wasn't in the cards for me to lose weight and get stronger. When I reflected back on what I had been doing, I realized I was tricking myself into thinking I was working hard. I was doing 20 push-ups in the morning before going to work, but I didn't have time to finish my full workout because I was running late, so I would tell myself to finish after work when I got home. When I got home I needed to do cardio, let me do my half hour on the elliptical machine, which I could do while watching T.V. Then the game would get too good and my favorite team couldn't possibly win unless I sat closer to the T.V. Then I was too hungry and tired to finish now, let me get my 10 push-ups in and take a shower and get something to eat. I'm glad I worked out because now I can have some dessert and bread and fried food because I worked out today and lost some weight and I'm not taking in more calories than I worked off. I was tricking myself into thinking that even if I stepped up my workout routine, I could still eat what I wanted, that diet didn't matter. I needed to stop tricking my body and my mind into thinking I was working hard. I wasn't committed; I would work out when I wanted to. I was interested in working out but certainly not committed. Part of being committed is having a mindset different than others or your old self. Muhammad Ali was once asked how many push-ups he could do. He responded "I don't know, maybe 15, 20." When he saw the strange looks his response received, as if he wasn't strong or wasn't working hard, he explained he didn't know because he didn't count push-ups from the beginning. He waited until it starts to hurt and then he would start to count. The 15-20 he did after it started to hurt was about the same amount I was doing <u>before</u> it started to hurt.

You may look the part; you may be going to classes in college but not studying. People see what they think you are achieving but someone else is beating you to the spot. One of the worst things that was said to me was, "If you would have just called me earlier I could have used you, I just hired someone." This was in response to me inquiring about a speaking engagement. This is worse than a "no" because I should have called that person a month earlier. I was denied because I was late to the party, because I went to bed without making one more call, send one more email or text. In this age of social media there is no excuse to not get a hold of someone. That will not happen again to me.

There are many barriers set up to prevent you from succeeding that are not in your control, the very least you can do is not be a part of the problem. It wasn't anyone's fault that I watched too much television, it's not anyone's fault that I went to sleep instead doing what needed to be done. Just like with pregnancy, as you become aware of being committed to your baby, the baby doesn't feed you, you have to feed your baby and the baby eats what you take in. Your goal that you're committed to feeds off of you, and if you don't feed it, well, I think you know what could happen. In an article I read from the internet entitled, "Ten Things Highly Successful People Do," one of the things successful people don't do is sabotage themselves.

4

"It is not because things are difficult that we don't dare. It is because that we do not dare that they are difficult." Seneca

The year was 1519; the man was Captain Hernan Cortes. His troops were some 600 men with about 16 horses and 11 boats. They had landed on what is today known as Mexico. Captain Hernan Cortes and his troops were attempting to do something that no one had done before, especially with his limited troops and resources. They were going to try and conquer the land of the Mayans. There had been other armies with larger number of men and supplies that had tried and failed this task before. Greater armies led by great nations wouldn't dare travel this far and not be prepared. To come this far with such limited resources was a death threat to this endeavor. So why would Captain Cortes come so far with such a small band of warriors?

Often times when armies set out on far away journeys, they would lose people to rough conditions, disease or storms along the way. So, while many armies would start out strong, they would most often reach their destination with as little as half of the troops and supplies that they began with. Maybe this was the case with Captain Cortes.

What could General Cortes have done that would have resulted in a different outcome? He could have gone back home and tried again or he could have sent a messenger ship back home and waited for help to arrive, but there was no guarantee that he or his troops would still be alive if and when help arrived. With the possibility of certain death in front of him and mutiny behind him, what could he do? He simply had to give one of his greatest commands ever; he simply told his troops to "burn the boats."

Motivational speaker, Les Brown, describes this situation in his YouTube video as, "Putting yourself in a position where you can't retreat." By burning the boats, Captain Cortes and his troop could not go back unless they gained victory. They couldn't retreat if things were going wrong, they couldn't retreat if the enemy was getting the upper hand, and they couldn't retreat if they were getting tired. By burning the boats, they only had two choices, die or victory. This is where you are now, you're committed and pregnant and there is no going back.

Lions are carnivores. They are meat eaters, and that's it. They know they don't' have the option of settling for eating plants if they can't catch their prey. They can't eat plants if the hunting of their prey doesn't work out. Their boats are burned; they have to eat what they are chasing after or they die. You have to burn your boat. You can't decide to quit if things don't work out or if you don't like the coach, or if no one is throwing you the ball or if the teacher doesn't like you, or the ever popular reason for quitting, "no one believes in me."

A lion can't retreat; it's the meat from its prey or nothing. The king of the beasts are not omnivores, they're not plant and meat eaters, to be committed or pregnant you have to go after what you're chasing with the mindset that I can't go back. This mindset puts you in the mood to want to work. How much work you put in may vary from day to day, but there has to be at least a minimum amount of work you invest on a daily basis towards your goal.

Sometimes people don't attack their dreams because they think that if they don't accomplish it, they can always do something else. If they don't make varsity; junior varsity is fine. If they don't get the lead in the school play, they're fine with the understudy. If you start with the attitude that you can always do something else, you will automatically be a step behind the opponent that can't retreat. There is no Plan "B".

This means you have to have an all-out commitment. Winston Churchill said, "Sometimes it is not good enough to do your best, you have to do what is required." By burning your boat, you will find yourself doing what you have to do.

I was standing with my uncle and my dad at a family reunion a few years after graduating college. My uncle said to my dad, "You have a good son." My dad said "Yeah." My uncle said, "You're proud of him, aren't you?" My dad said "Yeah." My uncle said, "But he knows if he has to, he can always come home, right." My dad said, "Oh no, he can't come back." This was my first lesson in burning my boat.

The comedian Bill Bellemy, in an episode of *Unsung*, talks about how he always wanted to be a comedian. He went to college and landed a great job. His employer believed in him and even paid for him to receive more schooling and paid him what he considered a great salary. But he wanted to be a comedian. So he put in the work, he did shows here and there, some small time shows in smoke filled rooms and even some bigger events like Def Comedy Jam which was aired on the cable entertainment giant, HBO. In a conversation with a friend, he was told that he wasn't a comedian until that was the only thing he did. He then quit his high paying job and did comedy full time.

Eric Thomas was in a similar situation. He was receiving what he described as a six figure income that he walked away from. He said it was tough to have to tell his wife that he was giving up not only his income, but the health benefits as well. He wanted to pursue his goal of helping people through his pet project of TGIM, Thank God It's Monday. He said he would basically record himself giving speeches, talking to people and trying to help them and doing it for free. Now his videos are one of the most downloaded videos on YouTube.

I know both situations are very scary. I'm not telling you to run out and quit your day job; you still have to have a plan. Burning your boat may be different depending on each person's situation, but now that you're pregnant with dreams and goals, you can't miss this step. If you're able to accomplish that while still working, more power to you. But when you commit to your goal, it will eventually commit back to you. Will Smith talks about how when you make a decision, a real decision about whatever it is you want to do, to do it undeterred, then the universe will get out of your way and things will happen for you.

My freshmen year at the University of Wisconsin-Parkside (UW Parkside) forced me into a situation where I had to burn my boat and I didn't even know it or realize it until I began doing research and reflection for this book. I had received a basketball scholarship after completing my senior year at Brown Deer High School. I was a 6'7" skinny beanpole that played basketball, baseball, and flag football during my middle school years. Baseball was my first love and I played it growing up in the summer for the Beckum-Stapleton Little League. It is now an iconic league that served thousands of youths in the Milwaukee area. I played the game, but didn't work at it. I later abandoned baseball when I got to high school because baseball was a summer sport that was played after school had let out for the summer. During the summer I decided to work instead as a caddy at a country club and I couldn't do both. So I chose work.

This is why I didn't try out for football as well, as it would cut in on my summer working time. Thus the only sport I could participate in was basketball. With this sport also, I played it, but didn't put in any extra work. I didn't work on my shooting, ball handling, conditioning, and was placed on the team mainly because I was tall and had showed the coaches some flash of potential. I even endured an episode of not making the varsity team my junior year and being told that if I wanted to play I would have to play at the junior varsity level. I wasn't a hard worker at the time, but I wasn't a quitter either.

I stayed on the junior varsity team even though younger players played ahead of me. I couldn't quit, even when another player in the same situation tried to recruit me to quit during a game. He said come on, let's just leave the beach. At the time I thought the coach just had it out for me and didn't want me to play, I now realize that I didn't deserve to play because of my work ethic or lack thereof. I was caddying in the summer but my attitude changed about working out to become better. I hadn't learned to burn my boat yet but I worked on improving my game. My work effort and commitment was linear, not exponential. While caddying and carrying a golf bag for 3-4 hours on a golf course, I would wear ankle weights. Ankle weights are small bags filled with sand that can weigh anywhere from two and a half pounds to five pounds. I started with the smaller size and worked my way up.

I would do jumping exercises and push-ups until I became stronger. I wasn't strong enough as a high school junior to lift even 80 pounds. I received a weight set as a Christmas gift and that gift turned into one of the most embarrassing moments of my life. One day while lifting in my room I put too much weight on the bar. If I had an older or younger brother he might have been my spotter. While lying down on the weight bench I was able to lift the weight off of the bar and into the air. I held the weight with my now extended arms over my chest area. I held it there for a few seconds as I envisioned lifting the weight. I lowered it to my chest and began to lift it back into the air to start my 3 sets of 10. "One," I counted in anticipation of getting the weight into the air. Only my arms and the weight didn't move.

I tried it again, "One." Still no movement from my arms or the weight, but I tried it a third time and fourth time, no movement. Come on Aaron focus, concentrate, and try it again. I tried it again this time yelling louder, "ONE." I was about to try it again, I couldn't give up, not because I was determined, but because if I couldn't lift the weight I couldn't get up either. I closed my eyes, my arms were burning now, pain was creeping in, visions of me dying while lying on the bench and being found days later crept into my mind. I had to be in this position for at least 10 minutes but it seemed a lot longer. I wasn't going out like this; I was not dying as a weakling that couldn't bench press the 80 pounds. I will win, let me get ready, let me count, "Two." Wait a minute, two, did I just lift the weight and am now on my second rep? I'm doing well, "Three."

Yes I had overcome, let me get to four, but instead of hearing the word four I heard something else. I heard another voice, a familiar voice. Where was it coming from? It was coming from above me, what was it? Was this an angel sent by God to help motivate me, to push me? Was the voice helping me count, the next number is five? Only the voice didn't say five, the voice said, "Ok, that's enough, next time lower the amount of weight until you get stronger." The voice was my mom who had heard me yelling out "One" and came to see what I was yelling about. She said she let me struggle as long as I could before she came to help me lift the weight. As if this wasn't embarrassing enough, I notice she only had to use one hand to lift the weight.

I began to get better but didn't push myself fully. I was a better basketball player my senior year, but still not great. I received more playing time than in the past but I could have been better if I had worked harder. Even though I wasn't a starter and not being recruited by anyone, I still had dreams of playing at a Division One school in college. I wasn't the best but was liked enough to be named one of the captains of the team and had told myself that whatever minutes of playing time I would get; I would play my butt off. I would run the floor as hard as I could until I fell out or was brought out of the game.

My attitude of not counting minutes played in a game, but making the minutes I played count is what led me to landing a scholarship opportunity. An assistant coach from UW Parkside, Dave Markesan, was in the stands watching another player at one of our games and he noticed me. He began recruiting me as a player with potential. I had to jump at that chance as my only other option was to join the Army Reserve. With that I red-shirted my freshman year, meaning I had to make all of the practices but wasn't allowed to play in games. It was a way for me to try and get better without losing a year of eligibility. Those days at practice were the hardest I ever had to endure because I was going against players that had already burned their boats, they wanted to play in the NBA, and they busted their tails and I was receiving training firsthand about how if two players that are equally talented are going head to head, the one who had worked harder would prevail.

I wouldn't had survived if Jeff Rhodes, a player from Milwaukee hadn't worked with me and showed me some moves and how to get my shot off against bigger, stronger players. He had given me the nickname of "A-Train" because in an attempt to get free to be able to shoot I would switch to shooting with my left hand to try and fool the defender. I went to the weight room with him and worked out in the pool. At the end of the season, when I thought I could rest, we still went to the gym and played. Those open gym times were tougher than practice because once you lost you couldn't get back on the court.

Because of the work I had put in, I finally was able to do something I couldn't do before; I could dunk. Not just a regular dunk, but I was throwing the ball off of the backboard and going up to get it. My legs got stronger and I was ready for the next year to begin.

At the end of the school season, all the players had to have an exit interview with the head coach. I and three other players were in the room at the same time and the coach talked about what each of us had to do to get better and how we could help the team. I remember my teammates laughing when he spent over 30 minutes telling me all of things I had to do to get better and how weak I was. I didn't care what others said because I was going to do the things coached demanded and had already started the process. After the meeting I talked to the coach about my dorm situation the following year. Because UW-Parkside was a commuter school, they didn't have dormitories on campus, students had to live elsewhere.

For me this meant living in an apartment with 3 other teammates and driving the 15 miles to school every day. My school and books were paid for but my parents paid my portion of the rent. For the upcoming school year, dorms had been built and players were getting their dorm assignments, fully paid as part of their scholarship. I didn't receive an assignment yet and knew it had to be an oversight. I asked coach about my dorm and he told me that he wanted to see how I played in the upcoming season before making a fully paid dorm a part of my scholarship. Not wanting my hard working parents to foot the bill for an apartment without roommates I said I needed my dorm paid. He said let's wait and see. This gave me a "why" for working out.

As school concluded in May, I didn't work at a job as much as I had in the past. I began to put more time and energy to working out and improving my game. Without realizing it, I had burned my boat. I was going to get my dorms paid for and wasn't expecting anything less. I ran at night to beat the heat, although the mosquitoes were a different problem. I went around to different parks and played ball all day, at Lincoln Park, Clover nook, Auer Avenue, and Green Bay. When I began dominating at certain parks, my cousin and I then drove to Chicago and stayed with my aunt and uncle and walked up to the neighborhood park to play. It took two days to get in a game as I wasn't known there and the players there didn't care who I was despite my height. When I was finally picked up I was going to dominate. I didn't have a choice because losing meant not returning. If you were going to beat me, you were going to have to break me. Will Smith said if he was on a tread mill competing against someone else, one of two things was going to happen, either the other person was going to get off first or he was going to die on that treadmill.

After a summer of improving I was ready to start my second year at Parkside. With that I had to talk to the coach about my dorm because my mother had been pestering me all summer about getting an apartment and getting ready for school. I told her everyday not to worry about my living situation because it was being taken care of. I met with the coach in his office and repeated my inquiry about the dorms and he repeated his decision about not paying for it. I stood my ground and said if my dorm wasn't going to be taken care of I was leaving. He made it clear that the choice was mine. Damn, I guess this is like when a girl breaks up with you and she says, "It's not you, it's me."

So for two weeks I was commuting back and forth from Milwaukee to Parkside, driving the 50 miles to Kenosha, pretending to be still in school. I had busted my tail that summer, getting ready, I had made a decision and if I couldn't get my dorm paid I would be playing for someone else. The only problem was that there wasn't someone else. Before signing with Parkside no one else had offered me a scholarship. I couldn't keep up with this charade, so I was set to tell my parents that I had basically dropped out of school. The night before I was going to tell them I received a phone call. It was from a coach at a Junior College in Montana, Glendive, Montana to be exact. He said he received a call from one of his players that played for him the previous year. In fact, the player was a classmate of mine who had graduated a year ahead of me from Brown Deer, Mark Bogan.

The coach stated that Mark had seen how much I had improved over the summer and was now a really good basketball player. He said Mark had told him that I was transferring from Parkside; I forgot that I had mentioned this to him one day while playing at the park. He wanted to know if I could send him some film of me and I said I didn't have any as my best basketball was done at the park. After an hour of talking he said based on the strength of Mark's word he wanted to offer me a scholarship. The next day instead of telling my parents I had dropped out of school, my speech I had practiced now turned into an announcement that I was transferring to the great state of Montana to pursue my educational goals. "Your gifts will make room for you." Proverbs 18:16 KJV

What burning your boat does for you is that it forces you to work harder than you probably ever thought you could. For some people there is something inside of them that keeps them pushing forward regardless of the situation, those are the one percenters. But for people like me, who the majority of us are, there has to be another source of pursuing and going after what we want, another driving force.

When I decided to become pregnant with writing this book I had burned my boat. I quit working other side jobs, I no longer drove for Uber, I had to dedicate any extra time I had to this baby of mine, my book. It's not easy, but nothing worth having is. There were many nights and days I would say writing this book is not bringing in any extra income, I should put it to the side for now. I wanted to quit so many times, but I couldn't, I had to keep going. However, in order to keep going, I needed some help. I needed someone to help me with this new process, this new baby. I needed what many of the great ones needed. I needed an OBGYN, someone more than just a doctor, but someone who often believed in me whenever I would waver or question the dream.

My OBGYN stands for **O**ften **B**elieving in your **G**oals when **Y**ou're **N**ot. The job of an OBGYN is to monitor you and the growing development of your baby, your commitment. You are supposed to have regular check-ups with your doctor much like women with an actual pregnancy. This person may be chosen by you or this person may come into your life at the recommendation of someone else. This person may or may not be different than the person with whom you partnered and committed with on your pregnancy goal. The person with whom you share your hopes and dreams and who is with you in your decision to make a commitment is the encouragement from the beginning. Remember they are your "Why Not" person.

This is not necessarily the difficult part of pregnancy, but possibly the most trying. At this point many women don't want to announce their pregnancy partially due to superstitious beliefs in case things don't work out, at this point you don't want the world to know what you're committed to because you don't have the strength to deal with the negative people and you want to keep moving forward.

Only a few select individuals should know about your commitment/pregnancy at this point because you want to spend your time working and not talking about it. Some people spend so much time talking about what they want and are going to do and not working at what they are going to do. With that in mind your OBGYN has to have three distinct qualifications. The first qualification is that he/she has to have either the experience of an expert in your field or have been through something similar to what you're about to go through. The second qualification is they have to be willing to be hated by you and not care. The third qualification is that they have to take your being successful personally. Without these entities, anyone that talks to you about what you are going through is only giving you their opinions, and not their advice.

In case you didn't know it, there is a difference. Anyone can give you their opinion. Opinions are a dime a dozen, everyone has one. Advice is different. Not everyone can give you advice. Advice is based on the knowhow of being an expert in a particular field. You don't ask your mechanic their advice on a law situation, you ask a lawyer. Advice can be given by someone who's been through it, whatever that "It" is. A lot of people will be happy to give you their opinion on how to start a business, but if they haven't started one, it's just opinion. If someone gives you the startup capital, they have a right to give you advice, or if their livelihood depends on your success, they can give you advice. If they are up at night with you and going through your morning sickness, they can give you advice.

Yes, you will have morning sickness. This comes in the form of regret. Regret for getting started; regret for ever thinking you could achieve the impossible. Regret for possibly quitting your job, or regret for not knowing things were going to be this tough. You have to understand that the reason the first trimester can be the roughest is because you have a life inside of you that no can see right now. No one, except for the few with your vision can see the changes you are making; others just want to see the finished product. My coach at UW Parkside couldn't see me working out, getting better in the summer. He didn't see the commitment I had to the baby inside of me.

He didn't see that I was getting stronger and could now shoot with an improved range. A young lady that ran track at UW-Parkside told me I should just quit trying to play basketball and try something else didn't see my baby it either. People may not see the results of the work you're putting in and may have nothing but a discouraging word for you. This is why you need to consult an OBGYN. Now remember, the OBGYN is someone who is checking on the development of your baby. Checking on you to make sure you're eating right, getting proper rest, and making sure pre-natal vitamins are taken.

This person has to be someone that can pester you and put a foot square up your a** when they need to. Yes, they will give you encouragement along the way but if all they are saying is, "Yes, you can do it," without making you do it, you'll just give in to the quitting or delaying what you need to do. This will lead to excuses for quitting.

Without my cousin forcing me to work out when I didn't want to I would not have had the strength to tell my coach pay for my dorm or I'm leaving. Some days my cousin, who was really my OBGYN, would have to cuss me out, talk about me, make me hate him so much, make me want to slap him so much, make me want to run him over with a car so much, that I worked out even harder just to shut him up. He didn't care how I felt about him; he just wanted me to accomplish my goals. That's why I love him.

My OBGYN in writing this book gets on my nerves. Always reminding me what I need to do or didn't do. Checking on the status of the book, editing, correcting mistakes, asking me what I meant by a phrase or how does a certain idea fit in. How nerve racking, so much so that I'm sitting here now at 2 in the morning typing this part. What the OBGYN will give you after determining that you are indeed pregnant, is something that all successful people must without a doubt have. The most important thing they will give you is a due date.

5

Cycles

"We are what we repeatedly do. Excellence, therefore, is not an act, but a habit." Aristotle

Ice cream with chocolate sprinkles and cherries on top with skittles on top of that. This may seem a bit nasty but mix this with crushed graham crackers and you will get what my sister loved to eat. Why would anyone in their right mind purposely want to eat that? Have you ever been around a pregnant woman? Pregnancy changes a woman's taste buds. Their taste selections become more unique and unusual. You will begin to develop cravings to do unique and unusual things too. For me, it became waking up in the middle of the night to write, not answering my phone as much, cutting out television and missing important football and basketball games in order to satisfy my cravings.

Let me pause a little bit to answer this question, "How do you know you're pregnant?" There are two things that will give you a clue if you're truly committed or have made a commitment to the point of being pregnant:

1) Your cycles stop
2) Your cravings begin

If you have cycles of starting and stopping something, cycles of always putting off until tomorrow what you should be doing right now, you're not pregnant. You can have all the best intentions in the world, but if you continually fall to the pressure of others to go out, skip the next workout or let others take care of something you should be handling, your cycle will continue.

But individuals that are truly committed stop cycles of procrastination and they begin to have cravings. They have cravings of wanting to do something else. Sometimes it's something else that doesn't make sense. You may have cravings to get up a little earlier than usual to get more accomplished. We all have the same 24 hours; you will start to get cravings to cut back on your sleeping and recreation hours to devote more time to your goal. Your cycle of going out with the crew will turn into cravings of not wanting to go with them. You will have cravings to work a little longer.

There are several different types of cravings, but one craving you must possess in order to succeed is the craving to create a plan. Successful people do not operate without a plan. If you want to start a business and borrow capital, a bank will ask for your business plan. This plan consists of having long term and short term things to do. Now it's important to note that I didn't write that you need to have long term and short term goals. I didn't make a mistake; you have to make plans, not goals. Goals are not plans; they are dreams that will become a nightmare without a plan. Coming from a former teacher and an educator's prospective, plans are a step-by-step process that you complete in order to achieve your goal. These plans run head-on into your due date.

Your short time plans are done daily and long term plans are done throughout a longer period like a week or a month. Notice I didn't say plans that expand a year from now. Your due date does not extend into a year. Making plans to accomplish something daily will stop cycles, we can't just leave things up to chance. By writing things down to complete by the end of the month, week or by the end of the day will put you on a schedule and get you into the habit of making and achieving due dates. This will help you from waiting until the end, and then missing the mark. If we don't set due dates, in order to compensate for falling behind, you add it on to your plans for the next week which turns into plans for the next month, and then next year. These plans will eventually turn into goals that don't ever get accomplished. Daily due dates come about because of your due date to give birth.

If you were to visit your child's classroom and ask the teacher what the students will be learning for the day, would you expect them to say I didn't plan anything for today but I plan on doing something by the time they graduate? You can't expect and demand things from others but not expect or make demands of yourself.

Your daily plans won't be easy to accomplish in the beginning but when your plans turn into cravings, you will find yourself not going to bed until it is finished or the very least attempted. These daily plans will stop cycles that contribute to not being successful.

In order to have success, you have to operate according to your plan, not to your emotions. These plans may be the same from day-to-day for a while but eventually they must change as you start to develop. Poor performances are born out of poor planning. To create a plan that will stop cycles, you have to create a plan that you are going to complete daily no matter what.

Your plans must include the following three core ideals:

- **Belief:** Your plans must be believable not only to you but to your OBGYN. Dreams should be unbelievable, plans shouldn't. I can make all the plans I want to about studying to become a doctor, but this won't work because it's not believable for me. I can handle seeing blood, but healing broken bones is out of the question, plus my hands aren't steady enough. This doesn't mean you shouldn't dream the impossible, like when man wanted to go to the moon.

In this case you have to transfer the unbelievable to believable. If you don't believe you can get something done, don't list it just to impress someone. You need to be real to yourself.

- **Desire:** You need to have the desire to enact what you say you're going to do. Don't get this confused with liking what you have to do. Not all athletes like the working out part but their desire to improve drives them to do it. I don't like getting up early to write a chapter but I desire the end results, so I do it. To me nothing great has ever been accomplished without desire.

- **Faith:** For some faith is the same as belief, especially belief in oneself. For me, faith and belief are not one and the same. Hebrews 11:1 (KJV) states "Now faith is the substance of things hoped for, the evidence of things not seen." In James 2: 17 (KJV) it states "Thus also faith by itself, if it does not have works, is dead. Unlike belief, faith is the work; you show your faith by how much you work. The greater your work or the amount of time you put in, the greater your faith. In Dr. Napoleon Hill's book, *Think and Grow Rich,* he say, "Hope is duty, not a luxury. To hope is not to dream... but to turn dreams into reality."

Belief, desire and faith are the essential parts for scripting your plans. Daily plans may be the same for a while. You don't necessarily have to come up with a new routine each day, but you have to follow what you plan.

Now you might say, "But I possess those things already and I'm still not having success with my plan." The reason for not having success with your plan yet is probably because you don't adhere to the next three steps:

- List the things that you will do no matter what
- List the thing/things you will may fail at today and do it any way
- Include a daily reflection

I must make my bed every day, because I like the way the bed feels when it's made. I then read bible verses and workout. I like to do these things daily but to be honest, there are some days that the bed goes unmade or I miss a workout, but no matter what, I don't miss brushing my teeth. Brushing my teeth is one thing that is so important that I won't miss it no matter what. That's how important the thing you will do no matter what must be. Not having a made bed is about comfort, but it won't determine how successful I am as far achieving my goals. However, while both are important to me, brushing my teeth has a direct effect on others.

Eric Thomas talks about until you desire something as bad as you want to breathe, you won't reach the next level. By listing the things you will fail at in your plans, you force yourself to try to set goals and plans that are unreachable and push you farther than you were the previous day.

Once this book is published I need to get out and have people purchase my book. Right from the start, I know that my momma is buying five. However, the next day, I need to get out there and sell to people other than family which will be scary and uncertain. I know that some people are going to reject the offer to purchase, but I have to continue to set goals that seem unreachable for right now. If my goal is to sell thirty books for a day, I may not get that. However, if I sell more books than I sold the previous day, I have achieved something. So I may have failed at reaching my projected sales, yet I still witnessed success.

The reflection piece determines whether you need to adjust your plans or if you are on target. Sometimes in your plans you may have set goals that are too small. If I set a goal of selling two books today and I sell ten, my goal was too low. If I set a goal of selling 100 books a day, that too may be an unreasonable goal. Reflection provides you with the opportunity to gauge your productivity based on reality while still reaching for more.

You're getting ready for the second trimester. For the first three months you have been preparing by immersing yourself into a commitment cycle. You're not worried about people recognizing the new you. The real critics have not surfaced yet because you haven't shown your transformation. Whether you know it or not some people like you in the state you're at, not succeeding, because it makes them look and feel better. The second three months is when there will be some announcement, a proclamation by you. Yes, even though I dropped out of high school, I'm going to get my doctorate degree. Yes, even though I don't have the financial backing, I will be starting my own business. Even though I have never been a starter in my high school career, I will get a division one scholarship. Your proclamation won't have to be vocal. Your presence may be the only announcement that's needed.

This is where Oprah can declare she will have her own talk show even when critics said she isn't made for T.V. This where Tyler Perry refused to be deterred even after his play failed to have any significant amount of success after several years. Get ready, you gift is about to kick you.

SECOND TRIMESTER

6

Evidence

They are literally, the few. Out of hundreds of applicants that apply only 2-3 candidates make it through the process. They are the proud. The position is for a volunteer program. It is one of the most difficult clubs to join. These few and proud are the members of the 3rd U.S. Infantry Regiment. They are responsible for guarding the tomb of the Unknown Soldier. The tomb has been guarded every day since 1937. This close knit group is not exclusive, but they don't just accept anyone. In fact, it's just the opposite; anyone with the guts to try can apply to make it into the club. What makes it so hard to join is the amount of work needed to become a Sentinel.

The tomb of the Unknown Soldier is guarded 24 hours a day, every day of the year no matter what the weather conditions are. They work in a rotation of 24 hours on, 24 hours off, 24 hours on, 24 hours off, 24 hours on, 96 hours off. They change every thirty minutes during the summer and every hour during the winter. During the time when the Arlington National Cemetery is closed, they change every two hours. Although this knowledge is known beforehand, individuals still sign up. They are considered the best of the elite 3rd U.S. Infantry Regiment, but they still are volunteers. How can this group of volunteers become the best? Let's take a small peek at what they endure for training.

Abraham Lincoln once said, "If I had eight hours to chop down a tree I would spend 6 hours sharpening my axe." In other words, Lincoln would spend 75% of his time getting prepared. It is said that an elite musician spends 90% of his time on practice or rehearsing and 10% of his time in actual performance. Even after the training the Sentinels go through; they spend a great deal of time rehearsing. When they are not on duty, they spend up to eight hours preparing to be on duty. This includes getting their uniform ready for inspection, taking care of their weapon, practicing their cadence and making sure their hair is cut a defined, particular way.

At this stage, the second trimester stage, you are in preparation mode. You are on 24 hours shifts.

You're on and then off, on and then off. You can't have a normal routine of working 8 hours, recreation for 8 hours, and then sleeping for 8 hours. Even when you are not working your shift, you are spending the majority of your time getting ready. You now are in the place where you are starting to show that you are pregnant. When a soldier volunteers to become a Sentinel, few people may know it. But once training begins, because that person is not going to be around old habits, people will notice a change. People will see some changes in you.

You are putting work into your gift. This cannot consist of you working regular hours. With this baby you may be up at 2 o'clock in the morning because an idea pops in your head. You may go to bed at 6 o'clock in the evening and get up at midnight. Hall of Fame basketball player Kareem Abdul Jabbar said in his book, *Coach Wooden and Me, Our 50-Year Friendship On and Off the Court*, while in college he used take a nap after practice and then wake up and study. For me, my sleep patterns were all over the place, but my body adjusted. I stayed up late and would then get some hours of sleep in and then get up to write. As the earlier stages of my book were written, my sleep pattern didn't too much matter. I wrote when and wherever, with the television on, kids in the background playing, phone ringing and even when my wife said she was sleepy I would say good night and continue to write in order to achieve my daily goal, but I didn't accomplish much.

But now in this trimester, my book is showing. As I got deeper into my pregnancy things shifted. I would pull out my plans and make adjustments, not to what I was going to do but the time frame in which I would do them. If kids were up I went to sleep, got up when they were in bed and checked on them and got to writing. The television time was cut out. My only television time was one hour of programing for pleasure and the rest of my viewing had to be shows that I had taped and could be used for research or for evidence portions of this book. Oprah Winfrey's life class, religious shows, certain interviews, were viewed and dissected. Because my pregnancy was showing, others would tape shows that they thought would contribute to my research so I could view it.

Adjustments weren't always easy. Sometimes going to bed meant going to bed when we had company. I would have to leave and go to my sister-in-law's house to get rest or to work on her computer. Sometimes I would have to get up 2 hours early before work. This meant I might be sleepy and still have to push through the next day. Commitment has no set time schedule. Yes, this can become uncomfortable. For a Sentinel, they have a creed that refers to the discomfort of the elements they have to go endure. You may need to develop your own creed to endure, whatever it takes.

Lena Patton, principal of Clark Street School in Milwaukee, said she refused to be comfortable. When she got too comfortable, she said she knew it's time to leave or change things up. The greats are comfortable at being uncomfortable. Like with a pregnancy, this is your baby and although it will be uncomfortable for a time, doing things that you haven't done before to be successful or to get to full term, is well worth the discomfort.

It is worth it for the Sentinels, otherwise they couldn't make it through the training. The dedication is what drives them. This is your dedication phase. This is where it starts to become more mental for you, than physical. Your gift will make room for you; your body will make room for the gift.

In a women's pregnancy her body will make some adjustments in the 2nd trimester. This is the time that morning sickness and fatigue begin to go away. Part of being fatigued is your body is not in the same shape as it was before, plus you are carrying and nurturing another person. In high school I could never seem to get in shape and was always tired while running sprints. Even when my body was in shape, my mind wasn't. Until I had the "why" I was doing something, I couldn't push myself.

For women that I interviewed, they stated this was the easiest trimester. They said that their energy level is up during this time and they are feeling better. This baby, this gift, this commitment, this dedication is growing inside of you. Their mind gets set not on what they are going through, but what they need to do to prepare for this arrival. What color do they paint the nursery, what name to give the baby, is the house child proofed, what school, daycare, hospital, clothes for the baby to wear home and a host of other things. Notice that the majority of the thoughts are not thoughts of complaints. My body doesn't complain anymore; it wakes me up. It pushes me. Since I became pregnant with this book, I no longer have to set an alarm clock. I haven't set one in over a year, even when it comes times to go to work. I don't need it because I am on 24 hour shifts now.

My editor has noticed my pregnancy. She says she wasn't sure about my completing this project before, but now she can tell that I'm pregnant. How could she tell? When I would submit work to her for editing I would have 1 to 2 pages for her to edit. And when she resubmitted them to me, it would take days for me to make corrections or days for me to talk to her about my thoughts on a passage that she didn't understand. Now she knows that I'm showing, because I began submitting 20 to 30 pages of writing at a time. I now call her the instant a resubmission is sent back to me. I don't end a conversion without setting a time for our next walk through of my work and I let her know how many pages I will have prepared for her next time. She even gives me research material and suggestions to put in my book. This is a part of why women say this trimester is easier, not easy, but easier, because people become more willing to help and assist you.

Again, by no means am I am saying that at any point things will be easy, it just becomes easier. What makes it easier? As people around you know you're pregnant, help comes. Not just help in the sense of people doing things for you, but the best help of all, the help of people getting out of your way. They don't offer you a drink at functions, they don't smoke around you, and instead they give you things that will help you. They offer their time and even may adjust their schedule to fit yours. Cedric Boyd, my former teammate turned author, is always offering encouragement by sending me ideas and resources that I can use for my book.

When my younger sister was pregnant she came to visit me at college, she was showing a little bit but you couldn't tell when she wore a coat. I took her to a social function and because she was family, people were accommodating and offering her a drink; before she could turn them down I stepped in and pushed it away. I remember one person saying that although she is my younger sister, she's not a child and she can have a drink if she wants to. I said she is pregnant and no more needed to be said. Once people know your situation further explanation is not always needed. Bishop T.D. Jakes also preached in a sermon that you should be able to see your destination by your preparation.

At this stage you began to have dreams, not just regular dreams of being successful, but dreams for your gift to be not just good, but the best. Mothers talk to their baby and begin at an early age to

7

The Work Within

"Silence your fears and doubts by facing the very things that scare you and challenge you." Joe Duncan

How does one make it through something that to others seem to be an impossibility or impossibly hard to do? We all have that quit factor in us. I know you hear from people that say I just don't quit. I used to say it also, but truth be told, I have a quit factor and so do you. There is a quit factor and what makes us quit is the fact that sometimes there may be things that are more important at the time. These are just illusions. Having to be the first at a movie premier is not a quit factor, however, my health or the safety of my family is a quit factor. In other words, as someone once said, if your reason for doing something isn't big enough, then your excuses will be. In your second trimester your reason for doing something has to lie within. This goal has now become a reality to you; it will allow you to push through the amount of work you have to do because you want to, not because you have to. When things to seem to get tough, your mind now automatically begins to focus on whatever you need to do in order to push through.

This new mindset is what makes a new Sentinel candidate make it through the training process. Each soldier must be in outstanding physical condition just to get to the interview process and persevere through a two week trial period to determine if they have the capabilities to train as a tomb guard. During the trial period, the trainees have to memorize seven pages of Arlington National Cemetery history. They have to be able to recite it on demand. It is after passing this portion that they are able to go to the new soldier training.

Not only do they learn the location of over 300 veterans and their grave sites, but they rehearse manual of arms, the guard-change ceremony, and the degree to which they have to keep their uniforms and weapons in immaculate condition. The next phase is to take a test that consists of 100 randomly selected questions out of the 300 items they are to know. They only need to score a 95% to pass. That means a 94% or lower is a failure. Not only that, but there are over 200 points of inspection in which you cannot have more than 2 minor infractions, this includes things like foot placement to cadence. This is done so that there is precision. They have to be precise because if they make it through and are given the honor of guarding the Tomb of the Unknown Soldier, there are no more dress rehearsals.

The guards walk the mat in front of the tomb and take exactly 21 steps. They then turn and face the tomb for 21 seconds, change their weapon to the outside shoulder, wait another 21 seconds and then take another 21 steps. They walk down to the other end of the mat and repeat the same sequence. They do this over and over again throughout their shift, morning, noon, and night, and in rain, sleet, or snow, winter, spring, summer, fall. They do this without the aid of a watch, a counter, or someone instructing them when to turn or telling them how many steps they have taken. They are able to fight through the fatigue and the pain of things getting too mundane. This pain and fatigue becomes a habit, afterwards it becomes a routine.

You will get to the point where you will be able to fight through what may seem to be the same routine over and over again without having any results because you know this is a process. You can't have a baby overnight. I know you heard about stories of an overnight sensation, but that is just a fallacy. Most overnight sensations have been at least ten years in the making. This is at least a 9 month process of putting in work, grinding day after day. You are starting to show, but you're not there yet. It's getting easier for you because you may have some rewards. You see some of the results. But this is not enough. I have some speaking engagements scheduled and a few chapters in my book completed, but that is not enough.

There is no quit in you not because it's not possible to quit, but because you are fighting for something. Even if you wanted to quit, you are at a point where your gift, your grind, your commitment won't let you. You become the life support system to your dreams. If you quit, your dream dies. Les Brown said in one of his several YouTube broadcasts, the richest place in America is the cemetery. He said the cemetery is where unwritten books by authors who didn't finish, lay there. Companies that should have been started by entrepreneurs that quit too soon lay there. New ideas that would have enhanced someone's life but never got started lay there.

Doing what you love feeds you in a way that keeps you looking forward. In looking forward you now need to make your scheduled check-up time with your OBGYN as part of your plan. Your plan that you fostered in the first trimester can be expanded and is now more specific. The things you can and will get done should increase because of your craving to accomplish the details you hadn't normally concentrated on in the past, which allows you to do more. You're not sleeping 8-10 hours a day. You're not wasting time doing unproductive things, the books you are reading are not just pleasure, they're about what can help and assist you to reach your goal. I love certain television shows and hate to miss an episode. But I put in as part of my original plan to cut back on certain shows and record others so that I can fast forward through them to cut down on the amount of time I spent watching television.

That was the first trimester, however as I began to approach full term, I had to make more adjustments. One of the secretaries at the school where I am the assistant principal likes one of the shows I watch. I stopped watching this show and began to get my information from him in the form of a summary. It takes about 5 minutes to hear an update. Is it the same as watching the show, no, but I'm showing now, my baby is more important than watching television. My habits have changed and the only way to change a bad habit is to replace it with a good habit. This is why my weekly scheduled time with my OBGYN is critical. Your scheduled time may be daily or multiple times a week. With an actual baby, a woman would not meet quite this often, but you schedule in your plans as often as needed.

Now, don't make the mistake of just thinking that you don't have to make it part of your plan because you can just meet here and there, or just have the doctor call when he or she has time or you can call them when you have time. How often do you just go to the doctor's office without an appointment? How often do you go the dentist without an appointment? Yes, you may have an emergency that comes up, but you generally schedule appointment times. Your professor at school has scheduled office hours as to when they meet with students. You must come at that scheduled time or make an appointment. I needed an appointment because I got tired of showing up at the block of scheduled time for my professor and have to wait in line behind 10-15 people. You must schedule a time that you will meet and put it in your plans because then you are holding yourself accountable to getting things done.

If you're so successful that you don't need help, then you probably wouldn't be reading this book, you would be writing it. All successful people have an OBGYN in their lives in some form or another to keep them on track. By scheduling a time, you have set a parameter for what needs to be done by that appointed time for not only yourself but for others around you. Sometimes people pull me in so many different directions that I can't get what I want or need to get done. But when I started showing in my second trimester, others started getting out of my way and began to push me forward. People would talk to me and turn the conversation towards my gift. So, how is the book going, how many chapters are you up to, are you still speaking? Others around you will start to be a part of what you are doing. They have begun to understand that the baby you are about to give birth to is real and ready to come out.

I have a cousin playing basketball for a major college. His team made the NCAA tournament and had the chance to make it to the Final Four. I met with him when his team came to town two days before game day. I talked with him the day before the game as well. On game day as his team ran onto the court to warm-up with some pre-game shots, my son and I were right by him and yelled his name. His mom was standing there as well and he didn't as much as turn and acknowledge us. Not with a smile, a head nod, nothing. Why? Because he was locked in to the game; he was getting ready to play. Were we mad and upset that he didn't respond to us? No, we knew he was pregnant and understood that he was about to give birth and that is where his focus needed to be.

When you schedule an appointment, it lets others know that you are not able to do anything else at that particular time. They won't bother you because you are locked in. When they call and you don't answer the phone or call them back right away, they understand. By scheduling an appointment, it forces you to get things done. I have to submit pages to my editor, my OBGYN; she reads the 15-20 pages and sends them back to me. She then calls me and says I have edited the pages and tells me when we will discuss some of the questions she has about my writing. It's not just about correcting the typos, but discussing what I am thinking for a particular passage, where am I trying to take the reader and did I mean to say what I have written. Before our appointed time I know that I need to have some other pages done to submit and have my other corrections done. It is the same as when you're at school or at work. Your teachers or professors give you a deadline. They don't say just get it done when you can. At work when your boss gives you a project, he/she needs it done by a certain time.

THIRD
TRIMESTER

8

Becoming Visual

"Indecision is the thief of opportunity" Jim Rohn

One of the greatest movies of my life time was *Rocky*, a movie that would span five additional sequels. The original *Rocky* and those that followed afterwards may not go down as one of the most epic pieces as far as cinematography, but once you know its origin, you realize that it can't be. It didn't stand a chance. Although the original *Rocky* movie would garner some seven nominations for an Oscar Award, which included: Best Actor in a leading role and best writing, (Sylvester Stallone), Best Actress in a leading role (Talia Shire), Best Actor in a supporting role, (Burgess Meredith and Burt Young), Best Sound and Best Music, the movie could never be held in the same caliber as the classic *"Gone with the Wind"* or the more modern day *"Titanic."*

Winning best picture, best director, and best film editing may not have secured *Rocky's* place in great film making history, but this doesn't matter because it is the story behind the movie that makes this movie great. I will elaborate on this in minute.

At this point in your pregnancy you don't know if your gift will allow you to say this is greatness inside of you, but you need to say it anyway. You need to talk to your baby daily. This is when you begin to talk to your baby about the dreams you have for them and what their future might hold. You talk to your baby about what they can aspire to be. Encouraging them to become President of the United States, or making a change or difference in the world, of becoming valedictorian, and whatever dreams you have for their unwritten script in the world.

You need to talk to your committed self the same way. You don't need to talk about the struggles, what can go wrong, what has gone wrong. You know that there are problems but you don't give life to them. You must focus on what sports psychologist, Dr. Bob Rotella, once said "All things are created twice, first **visually** and then **physically**." This is where you give in to your visual. You have to see it, before you see it, in order to see it. Your vision of what you see for the future will have to carry you through because even though you are showing signs of getting to where you want to be, you haven't given birth yet. You are showing and things are starting to maybe happen for you, but you still have a ways to go. Talking to yourself will take you through even further than your planning will. Your daily plan helps make you productive, but now productivity is not enough.

As others witness your productivity they may start to offer you something that makes you fall short of what you set out to do. Others may try to tell you what you have is good enough, you don't have to rewrite, you don't have to get another degree, what you have is just fine. Remember, others don't have your vision, they don't see your blue print of where you're going. They know that you're pregnant, but so are a lot of other people. You may not have separated yourself from the rest of the field yet. You may get offers, but those offers may fall short of what you set as your goal to be. This is what happened to Sylvester Stallone, this is what made *Rocky* so great. This is where *Rocky* might not have ever morphed into the sequels that followed. For me, it is the story of *Rocky's* birth that made it one of the greatest films of all time.

Broke, no money, hungry, needing to pay rent, unable to feed both himself and his dog, Sylvester Stallone did the only thing he could do. He sold his dog, for twenty-five dollars to a stranger he met at a local liquor store. The dog was more than just a dog; he was his companion when he lived in New York. Butkus was his best friend, but he was broke, so broke that he hocked his wife's jewelry. She would later become his ex-wife. As broke as he was, he still had a dream, he wanted to act. His lack of money made him go to the library to keep warm. While there, he stumbled across the poems of Edgar Allen Poe and became inspired to want to write and act as well.

Fortified with this new ambition he and Butkus move to California where they lived in a one room flat that Stallone says he was able to open the window and the front door while lying in bed. It is here, in California, that he sold his dog, his friend. He tried to get fifty dollars for him but had to settle for twenty-five. At the time I'm sure Stallone didn't realize that he had become pregnant. His dream was inside of him and he had become committed to the degree of pregnancy.

Sylvester Stallone watched a fight between Muhammad Ali and Chuck Wepner. He was impressed how this overmatched opponent of the great Muhammad Ali wouldn't quit, lasting all fifteen rounds and even managed to knock Ali down. It inspired him to write the script for *Rocky*. He had completed only about 80% of it when he went to an audition. He didn't get the part, but on the way out of the door he asked someone at the audition if they would be interested in seeing his script. They took it and liked it; liked it enough that they made him an offer to buy the script. They offered Stallone $25,000. Wow, Stallone is about to go from having to sell his dog for twenty-five dollars to a stranger to being offered $25,000 at one time for a script he was inspired to write after watching a heavy weight fight.

It wasn't a script that came about as a result of some kind of life's work, it wasn't a 10, 15, 20 year journey to get this script written, sold and made into a movie; it was a script that came about by the inspiration of a poem. He didn't even know what he was doing. I would have been excited and took the offer, but he didn't. Instead of simply taking the money, he told them that in order for them to buy the script and make the movie, they had to fulfill one obligation, he had to be in the movie, and even more, he had to play the part of Rocky. The studio said no can do. They said they already had other actors in mind to play the part of Rocky. They had veteran actors Ryan O'Neil, Robert Redford, Burt

Reynolds, and James Caan in mind. Certainly Sylvester Stallone couldn't argue with that, could he? He could and he did. He stood his ground and said he had to play the role of Rocky.

The producers must have really like the script because they sweetened their offer and raised it to $375,000. Now, the pressure was on, he had to take this offer. With this offer he could go buy his dog back, move to a bigger place with more than just one bedroom. He could afford not to work and possibly begin writing another script. But unknown to the producers, Stallone's baby was growing inside of him. He couldn't say yes, his baby was to play the role of Rocky. He would later say that he would never forgive himself if his movie turned out to be a hit and he didn't insist on playing the lead role. He turned down their offer.

The producers came up with a final offer. He could play the role of Rocky in the movie, however, their $375,000 offer was now back to $35,000 and they would only give him one million dollars to produce and make the movie. A million dollars to make a movie was unheard of. Sticking with his unwavering stance to be in the movie, he took the offer. He took the $35,000 and made the movie for just under the million dollars. He shot the movie in the Philadelphia area with mostly a hand held camera. There were scenes that were shot so economically that Stallone stated that he would be riding in a car with the director and he would tell him to get out and start running. Sometimes he was instructed to just run as fast as he could, and he ran until he legs felt as if they would fall off.

Because of the low budget, compromises had to be made. In the script where it had called for extras or a multitude of people, he had to change things where there would be just two people or film with a lot of his friends standing in. He even had a part for one of his best friends, his dog Butkus. But in order for him to be in the movie he had to get his dog back. Before he left for Philadelphia to film the movie, he went back to the place where he sold his dog in hopes of running into the person he sold it to. He searched and waited three days before finding the new owner. He told the guy how much the dog meant to him and he was willing to buy the dog back for $100. The guy said no. Then Stallone raised the offer to $500, still no. The new owner of the dog even turned down a $1,000 offer from Stallone. They eventually reached an agreement and settled on $15,000 for Butkus. That's almost 43% of the $35,000 he received for his script.

Who would pay so much for a dog? Who would turn down $25,000 when you are living in a one room place where you can open the window and the door while still lying in bed? No one would certainly turn down $375,000 as a final offer. Who would turn down all of this, for just a part in a movie that is not even guaranteed to be successful? Who would do this? Sylvester Stallone would, and you would have also because at this stage you're in your third trimester and you're showing signs of getting ready for birth. Stallone didn't cave in to the pressure of what he truly wanted to do and you know what, you won't either, not when you have your goal growing inside. You will have opportunities to stop or quit just short of what you really want, that is guaranteed. However, your desire to go full term will take over your desire to fall short of what you originally planned for.

At this point you will have to make a hard decision to give into the comfort zone. Successful people are comfortable at being uncomfortable. Harriet Beecher Stowe said, "You are to never give up, for that is just the place and time that the tide will turn." You won't give up if you understand the principal that Stallone followed.

Chapter 9

Feeding Your Gift

"Stop thinking in terms of limitations and start thinking in terms of possibilities." Bob Proctor

What did Sylvester Stallone do that allowed him to stick to his demand of portraying Rocky in the movie? He had five things that you must process now. These things are only for those close to giving birth, ready for their water to break and ready for things to break in their favor. This is where opportunity meets hard work; another name for this opportunity is "luck."

The first thing Stallone made was an investment, an investment to himself. This may be the point where others liken to making a decision. While I do believe it's true, that making a decision can be the first step toward heading for success, if you don't make an investment in yourself you can easily decide to do something and have that decision exist only in your mind. Here is something to think about. Human beings value, value; they value things that are or seem valuable. I am reminded of a joke in which a man was trying to get rid of an old refrigerator. He set the fridge on his front lawn with a sign that stated FREE, PLEASE TAKE. For two weeks no one took it. He then changed the printing on the sign, FRIDGE, $50. It was stolen the next day. You will value, value, by investing in yourself. You must value yourself more and deposit more into yourself.

When Sylvester Stallone packed up his limited belongings and moved from New York to California with no place to stay or job, he made an investment. Jack Canfield, the co-creator of the all-time best selling *Chicken Soup for the Soul,* talked on Oprah's *Super Soul Sunday* television show about how he maxed out his credit cards in trying to publish and promote his book. The more you invest the harder it is to quit or give up. No matter how much you believe in what you want to do, you're going to have some doubts. Even if you're doubts are the size of a mustard seed, there are doubts none the less. But what you put in, or invest, will help carry you through. *Chicken Soup for the Soul* turned into a series of books that sold over 500 million copies. It didn't start out as a great seller; Canfield was turned down over 140 times. Was it his belief that kept him going or the amount of investment he put in the book that kept his belief going?

The second thing Stallone did was he turned down immediate profit to hold out for what he really wanted. He turned down good to be great. He didn't just want to be pregnant, he wanted a baby. Yes, it must have been hard to turn down $375,000 for the future. Stallone didn't have hit movies before *Rocky* that he could fall back on. He could have said let me sell this script and then I'll keep the next movie until I can act in it. He could have even negotiated a part in the movie other than the lead role. What are you willing to give up now for future success? Yes, it's easy to give up something when you don't have anything. In your third trimester, you can see the light. When you started you had to have a vision because you couldn't see things with your sight. Things were not visible for you. Before Tyler Perry became successful he had to use his vision because with his eye sight he didn't see a mansion, he saw the car he was sleeping in.

According to Tyler Perry when he appeared on *Oprah's Master Class*, even when he produced his first stage play, he didn't have a big audience or packed theaters. It could have been easy for him to sell himself short, but he persevered and held on. Eventually he started selling out his plays in multiple cities, it took him 7 years, he now had something to lose, and he had something to give up for the future. Eric Thomas walked away from his six figure job with health benefits for something that wasn't there, but allowed him to do what he needed to do in order fulfill his purpose.

There were many days after I got a promotion at work I wanted to say the heck with this book, I'll just put my time in and try to get the next promotion. I was tired of being sleepy and tired of missing out on the things I liked to do. Currently I'm on page 70 of this book and it's the middle of March Madness, the time of the NCAA Tournament and I'm missing some great games. North Carolina beat Kentucky by two points on a shot with .03 seconds. Florida beat the Wisconsin Badgers on a last second 3 point shot after Zak Showalter, a guard on the Badgers; hit a running one-legged 3 pointer to send the game into overtime. I had to read about it in a text from my son. I had to see my kids celebrating the North Carolina win through social media. But since I'm so far into the book, I have to give all that up now for rewards later. I'm too close to giving birth to my finished book.

The third thing that Stallone did, he had to pay the price for what he wanted. In this case he paid a significant price for his dog. When he found the person he had sold his dog to, he said the dog meant so much to him. He showed how much with the amount of money he paid for the dog. Spending $15,000 to get the dog back is not about the amount of money, it's about how much are you willing to spend to get what you want. It's one thing to give up something, like sleep, but it's another to give up money that you need. Someone said you can tell what a person wants by what they spend; check your credit card statement, your checkbook, your accounts payable to see what you want.

I'm frugal, some people call me cheap. But I'm not cheap when it comes to getting something I really want. Now that I'm pregnant with this book, I am willing to spend for it. I can't buy other things, the new shoes that I not only want, but need; I can't get the new suit or tailored shirt that would match another suit. I have to spend money on this book and the things that are involved in it. Editing is not cheap, checking for mistakes and the walkthroughs of making sure what I was trying to convey actually was communicated after checking in with my editor. The cost of doing research and collecting material, printing paper and the inability of making more money doing other jobs because this is my baby now, I can't put it down.

Most importantly I am willing to spend my time, how much time are you willing to spend? The fourth thing Stallone did was he made do with what he had. He filmed the movie with a hand-held camera, and he used a lot of his friends as extras in the movie because he couldn't afford to pay actors with his limited budget. He shot scenes with people in the background that had no idea they were a part of the movie. Stallone talked about certain scenes where he is running and people are just reacting to him thinking he is some crazy, running guy. They're throwing things at him and he catches them and throws it back. He had a limited amount of time as well, but he made due. The weather didn't always cooperate, but he made due.

Not having certain things that you may or may not truly need cannot hinder you. This is where your visits to your OBGYN are most valuable. All authors need an editor. Editors charge a certain amount per word. The person editing this book for me is very valuable, but not a professional editor. My editor gives me the best she can as to insure that this book gets done regardless. This is where your plan becomes most crucial. The third trimester should start to yield you some dividends. It's easier to keep going when you see some of the rewards and some monetary things may be coming your way. But here you can't let what you don't have keep you from getting what you want. Stallone was able to get the film done in a month, yes, that's worth repeating, got it done in a month. No excuses, no waiting for a better time, no waiting for more resources.

On your visits to your OBGYN it is necessary for you to get an ultrasound. This allows you to see what you can't see. Your ultrasound picture will give you stamina when you're tired. I came home from work very tired. I had planned on working on my homework for a class I am taking, which was due in two days. Yes, along with working a full time job, writing this book, working to get speaking engagements, I have to take a class which will give me another Master's degree for the promotion I received. Needless to say, I'm very tired. My pastor commented the previous Sunday, "Man you must have more hours in the day than others because I don't know how you have so much to do and manage to get it done." I don't have more hours, but in studying successful people I do what they have learned, I make better use of the same amount of hours that everyone else has.

So when I woke up at 10:30 p.m. after falling asleep at 8:00 p.m. I couldn't go to bed. I contemplated simply going back to sleep and getting up at 3 a.m. the next day, but then I wouldn't accomplish one of my must dos on my planning list. I must write something every day, no matter what. Yes, I could write at 3 a.m., but that would be the next day, I had to make use of what I had, which was another hour and a half to get something written. Doesn't matter how many pages, I had to write something.

You will want to cut some corners and give in to the temptation to put off until tomorrow what you can do today, but two things at this stage in you pregnancy will help you to make use of what you have. One, pull out your ultrasound picture; this is what I did before I wrote. What is the ultrasound? It is the picture of whatever you're striving for and beyond. For me it's not just one ultrasound. I have a picture on my phone of a house that has everything I dream of. Notice, I didn't say a house of everything I need or want, but a house I dream of. This picture has screen shots of several different rooms, there's a screen shot of the office within the house I dream of, the man cave and the cars that go in the four car garage. Will I buy this house when I give birth to this project? That's irrelevant. However, being able to have that as an option is extremely relevant. You don't want regular dreams. If you have a dream that is within reach right now, then you're not dreaming enough or big enough.

Your dreams should be something that one, only you can get accomplished with the help of God and two, makes people laugh. While working with students at my school, poet and speaker Kwabena Nixon had several of my male students he was working with write down their dream. He said that young people without a dream don't have hope. I noticed that one student wasn't writing down anything. I went and sat next to him and asked why he wasn't writing anything. He said that he doesn't have a dream. I asked him are you sure you don't have anything you would like to become or have in the future. He said no and then asked me what my dream was. I told him that I had several and one of them would be to have a private plane. He immediately began to laugh, and then I said because you're laughing, my dream must be good.

When I pull out the picture of my dream, my ultrasound, I talk to it. I talk until I get a clear vision of what I want. This vision then allows me to move into action and to do something. This talk to your baby, your commitment, your gift, is fuel for you. I have read stories of how even some of the most underprivileged individuals talk to their babies about things they can accomplish and the things they can be. Slaves, not knowing the ending of their slave lives, talked to their children about how great they will become. Even in their conditions, they managed to be encouraged. This allowed slaves to learn a language without formal schooling. Slaves had to keep their tired bodies up and learn to read by candlelight at night, as learning and showing they could read could get them whipped or cause their death. They took a chance because they looked at their ultrasound and dreamed big, stupid, unheard of dreams.

These dreams allowed Harriet Tubman to push forward and free slaves through the Underground Railroad. These dreams allowed her to push forward even though many slaves she was trying to free from bondage did not want to go. This allowed her to push forward even when after freeing her brother, he decided to go back to slavery. This allowed her to push forward even after returning from freedom to rescue her husband, she discovered that not only did he not want to go, but he had remarried someone else. She pressed on.

From this talking to your gift, something amazing happens. Your gift will kick back. To feel the foot of my baby while in the womb kicking back at me brought me unspeakable joy. Even though this may be of some discomfort to a woman, she doesn't focus on the discomfort because of what is moving in her. Right now as I am typing, I am uncomfortable; I am truly tired and ready for sleep. It's late but my baby is kicking, I'm ready for bed, and then my wife comes out of the room to see where I am, why I haven't come to bed. She sees me typing and comes over by me and instead of saying its late, go to bed, she feels the baby kick, she starts to read for the first time what I have been writing. She sees the number of pages I've typed on the page indicator. She reads some more. Then she points to something and corrects a mistake, the baby is kicking, she feels it and smiles. I can write for another two hours.

The fifth thing that Stallone was willing to do was expose himself. Yes, at this point you're exposed, no longer hiding it, people can see you're pregnant. I had to expose myself as a writer. I don't have a book out yet, but I had to expose my writing to others, others that will give an opinion on what I wrote and for me this is one of the scariest things of my pregnancy. Before his movies hit theaters, Stallone showed his film at a screening for the Director's Guild in Hollywood. Along with his mother there were over 900 people from the film industry in attendance. In an interview he said it didn't go well, people were not laughing where he thought they should be laughing and the fight scenes didn't get any response. After the showing, a dejected Stallone told his mother that he would come back home and get his life together and get a job.

There would of course be no need to do that with the success of his movie. For some reason all of the feel good reception you receive at the start, at the conception stage and first trimester turns into negative. This is where people remind you of all the pain you are going to face when you give birth, all of the complications and what could go wrong. When I sent out excerpts of my book to friends and family members, I exposed myself to people telling me how much I had to endure from all of the mistakes I had in my book, how hard it would be to get it published and even if I did how hard it would be to make any money. How the concept of the book didn't make sense, which was funny because when I talked about the concept of the book in the early stages to a few people that asked me about it, they said it was a great idea and couldn't wait for the book, now that I'm close to giving birth, a different story is being told to me.

Yes, I know not everyone is going to like what I wrote, yes, I know about the percentage of books that are written yet never make it to publishing. Yes, I know that even after getting published, books can sit in warehouses forever and gather dust. I know about all that can go wrong not because I sought out the information, but because of exposure, all of this information was told to me. But the pain of what was to come couldn't deter me. I feel the baby kicking and I know it's almost time for delivery. Although I have a due date I don't know when my water will break. I have a due date for the completion of my book, but I don't know when my water will break for the publishing. I don't know when my water will break for the title of the book. I don't know when my water will break for the concept of the cover jacket. Do I use a picture of just me, me and my family, or no picture at all?

I know my due date, but when will my water break? Who will do the forward, do I write the forward and asked someone to just sign their name? Do I ask a friend or try to get someone with a little clout? Sorry if I sound nervous now but I'm close, you will be just as nervous as you become closer to your goal. Will the pain be too much, the pain of rejection? Rejection is easy in the beginning, but I poured too much into this. How do I deal with the pain after my water breaks? Some women want a natural child birth, but others choose an epidural to help with the pain. I also make use of an epidural to help with the pain.

Don't get me wrong, rejection hurts, someone telling you "NO" or letting you know that you're not good enough is painful and I don't want to sit here and simply say get over it or you have to be tough. You do have to get over it and be tough but what I learned is that successful people feel pain as well. I don't want to put anyone on the spot but you have no idea how many ultra-successful people have had a good cry or experience episodes of screaming and yelling and wanting to quit or beat someone up. Think about this, even Jesus asked his Father if he could take this cup, this burden from him. I have learned that it's okay to feel pain, especially now that it's time to give birth. Don't worry about trying to mask the pain, take your epidural.

I have two epidurals as I am in the process of pushing this book out. The first epidural is me singing in the shower. I sing, well, if truth be told, I can't sing, but in the shower you can't tell me any different. I sound like Brian McKnight. I can sing so well that I can ease any pain that I am feeling, nothing can touch me at that time. I can sing all of the blues away. I can hit every high note, low note, and notes in between, but to me I can do the impossible in my singing. No's, aren't no's, when I sing. Rejections aren't rejections when I sing, not good enough is great when I sing, as long as it is in the shower.

When I'm done you would think that nothing can touch me or bother me. My pain is gone and I'm ready. If that doesn't work or I need a little more pain relief, I can use my second epidural. I put on my headphones and dial in a slew of motivational sound tracks and go do something. I don't just sit around and listen. I have to be doing something, movement, like cutting the grass, shoveling, or working out. Whatever I am doing I have to do it in isolation; alone. I don't want anyone talking to me. While listening I'm firing myself up so I can't be around people, especially my kids, because I may have to shout, yell, or say an occasional cuss word. Sometimes I my cuss myself out, in some instances, I may be telling myself that I can do it at others times I may be telling myself to quit crying, quit being a baby, get my lazy a$$ up and get to work.

At the point when your water breaks your only focus is to get your baby out. It's been long enough now, it's time to push. When you don't feel like it, push. When the pain is unbearable, push! My due date is approaching, I will send this book to the publisher by May 27, 2017, Memorial Day weekend and I'm too close. Nothing else matters. This is hard because this means I have to be unbelievably selfish. Selfish to the point that others around me get mad at me for not answering their phone calls, their texts, emails. That's okay because they know I'm pregnant and if they don't understand my water has broken, too bad. When a woman's water breaks, do you think she is worried about her regular day activities? My time is running out and my due date is right around the corner. As Eric Thomas says, I can, I will, I must. This is my last chapter of this book but I have to go back and do some rewrites, so I can't worry about anything else.

I have spent too much time wasting it before. No more, I'm pushing. This pushing is hard work; I have to push with all of my strength, blood, sweat and tears. I am at the end and can see the delivery of my book, my dream. It took a lot of hard work but now I know it was worth it. It was tough but worth it. Minister T.D. Jakes states in one of his sermons, "You are trying to deliver something that will deliver you." This explains how hard this part is and yet rewarding at the same time because at this point you're trying to deliver something that is going to deliver you.

Yes, this book will deliver me, it has delivered me from thinking that there is nothing that I can't accomplish. Putting this book together was one of the most difficult things I ever had to do. Was it worth it, was it something I would do again, was it was something that I would put myself through again? Do I really want to keep pushing and pushing? It hurts, like a woman going through the birthing process I scream and yell.

Malcolm X says he learned that if you want something in life, you had better make some noise. This book, my giving birth, is my making noise. I'm letting it be known that I am here; I'm going to be noticed. What will my baby grow up to be, I don't know, but I do know my commitment will grow. How do I answer those questions above? I'll just answer the questions by saying I have already begun to prepare to give my new baby a sibling.

Resources

Below is a list of some of the sources I used for research to gather my thoughts and determine the pathway I wanted to pursue while writing this book. However, there were numerous other quotes, YouTube videos, video clips, webinars and TED Talks that inspired and pushed me to birth this dream.

Abdul-Jabbar, Kareem. *Coach Wooden and Me, Our 50-Year Friendship On and Off the Court.* Grand Central Publishing, 2017.

"The Amazing Story of the Making of Rocky." *The Amazing Story of the Making of Rocky*, Wordpress, 24 Nov. 2011, www.almorel.com/2011/11/the-amazing-story-of-the-making-of-rocky/.

Becker, Jill. "Shaping Sara Blakely: Meet the Billionaire Founder of Spanx." *Entrepreneurship*, 7 Dec. 2015.

"Michael Jordan Failed Over and Over and That is Why He Succeeded." *Passion Meets Purpose*, FeelingSuccess, 20 Aug. 2015, www.feelingsuccess.com/michael-jordan-failure/. Accessed 14 Jan. 2017.

If your organization would like to book Aaron Womack Jr., please
contact him at: atrainwomackjr@yahoo.com - (414) 841-1447.